Dear Fruly,

Keep on open mind and
heart and who knows

The Law of
Divine Compensation

what can happen!

love

Lauren

The Law of Divine Compensation

On Work, Money, and Miracles

Marianne Williamson

HarperOne

An Imprint of HarperCollins*Publishers*

HarperOne

HarperCollins books may be purchased for educational, business, or sales promotional use. For information, please e-mail the Special Markets Department at SPsales@harpercollins.com.

HarperCollins website: http://www.harpercollins.com

HarperCollins®, ♨®, and HarperOne™ are trademarks of HarperCollins Publishers.

FIRST HARPERCOLLINS PAPERBACK EDITION PUBLISHED IN 2014

Library of Congress Cataloging-in-Publication Data
Williamson, Marianne.
The law of divine compensation : on work, money, and miracles /
Marianne Williamson.
p. cm.
ISBN 978–0–06–220542–1
1. Wealth—Religious aspects. 2. Spiritual life. 3. New Thought.
4. Providence and government of God. 5. Money—Religious aspects.
I. Title
BL65.W42W55 2012
299'.93—dc23 2012028284

21 LSC(H) 20 19 18 17 16 15 14

The most important decision we make is whether we believe we live in a friendly or a hostile universe.

—Albert Einstein

CONTENTS

PREFACE

Few areas of our thinking, or our circumstances, can be more stressful than work and money. The late actress Sophie Tucker is credited with having said, "I've been rich and I've been poor, and believe me, rich is better." Most people would agree.

At a time when the institutional processes normally counted on to support our financial good have gone south, if not completely haywire, many people are looking for alternative routes to economic security. We want to work, but can't find work. We want to invest, but don't feel we can do so safely. We want to have enough money in the bank, and find ourselves terrified at the thought that we might not.

It is often at the moment when our way isn't working anymore that we open our minds to consider something new. Finance is just one of many areas where an increasingly obsolete, materially based worldview is proving inadequate to the challenges of the times in which we live, and more and more people are finding practical wisdom in spiritual understanding. Dogmas and doctrines—both religious and economic—are being left behind as a deeper realization of the power of consciousness and its primacy in the creation of human affairs becomes a more popular avenue to a happy life.

Spiritual truth is expressed in many forms, both religious and secular. I have been a student of a set of books called *A Course in Miracles*—a self-study program of psychotherapy based on universal spiritual themes—for thirty-five years. As a teacher of the principles of the *Course,* I've had the opportunity to witness as well as experience their practical applicability. The crux of the *Course,* which is not a religion and has no dogma or doctrine, is the relinquishment of fear and the acceptance of love into our hearts to replace it. I've seen miraculous transformations occur when we change the nature of our thinking from fear and limitation to faith and love.

From a metaphysical perspective, every experience begins with a thought, and our experience changes when we change the thought. If we have a problem in any area—whether relationships, health, money, or anything else—the first place to look for a solution is in the nature of our thinking. This applies to money no more and no less than it applies to anything else.

This book is a guide to spiritual principles that pave the way to material abundance. These principles are based on my understanding of *A Course in Miracles*. Theory alone does not change our lives, but theory activated by mental shifts and behavioral follow-up becomes nothing short of miraculous help in even the most troubled times.

THE MAIN PRINCIPLE of *A Course in Miracles*, and key to the peace of God, is this: "Nothing real can be threatened. Nothing unreal exists." Love is the all-encompassing reality of God and thus can have no opposite. The absence of love, which is fear, is mere illusion. Love is the only eternal truth, while fear is a hallucination of the mortal mind.

Throughout this book, the fear-mind will be referred to as the ego.

Every thought is a cause that produces an effect. According to *A Course in Miracles,* every thought we think creates form on some level. If your mind is in a loving place—if your thoughts are of a high, divine vibration—your experience will reflect that. If your mind is in a fearful place—if your thoughts are of a lower, dense vibration—your experience will reflect that. The way to change the nature of your experience is to change the nature of your thoughts.

Seeking to solve a problem merely on the level of effect is not a true solution but only a temporary fix. Only when we address the level of cause—the thoughts that caused the original deviation from love—do we produce miraculous and fundamental results. By remembering what is real while in the presence of the unreal, we miraculously transform a problem on the level of its cause. A miracle is a shift in perception from fear to love—from a belief in what is not real, to faith in that which is. That shift in perception changes everything.

In our ability to think about something differently lies the power to make it different. Miraculous thinking does not represent a state of denial, at least not in the traditional sense. It doesn't represent the magical thinking of simply looking away from something horrible and pretending it doesn't exist. If anything, it is a state of *positive* denial: looking at something and knowing that since only love is ultimately real, nothing else has ultimate effect. The miracle-worker does not look away from the illusions of the mortal world but rather looks *through* them, thus invoking a world that lies beyond. This book is not about denying our economic problems; it's about transcending them. It's about realizing that illusions—no matter how entrenched they might be within the three-dimensional world— cannot stand in the presence of love.

Through the authority of loving thought, we are given the power to turn any situation that is not love back into love, starting with thinking about it differently. We do this by identifying our own love-lessness and being willing to let it go. Thinking this way—which is sometimes easy, sometimes not—is the mental habit of the "miracle-minded."

God has introduced into our minds an Internal Teacher, authorized to help us cross the bridge from fear to love when we find it difficult to do so by ourselves. The Internal Teacher is called by different names, from the Comforter, to Jesus, to the Holy Spirit. Whatever name we use, it cannot be called on in vain. Miracles are a divine intercession from a thought system beyond our own, bringing inner light into a darkened world.

And miracles are summoned by conviction. Conviction can be seen as an attitudinal muscle that gives us strength to see beyond appearances and invoke the possibilities that lie there. With God's help, our own particular worldly veil of illusion—whether it takes the form of bankruptcy, recession, or any other form of fear—is lifted, and we can see beyond it. No matter what our problem, or its form or size, an infinite field of miraculous possibility awaits our open-mindedness and love. "Miracles occur naturally as expressions of love," according to *A Course in Miracles.* This book is about money, miracles, and love.

SOME PEOPLE MIGHT read this book and say, "Oh yeah? Well what about starving children in Africa? Are they poor because their consciousness is unaligned with love?" I'd like to take this opportunity to respond to that.

Starving children in Africa are not poor because their consciousness is unaligned with love; they're poor because ours is. A billion people on earth live in "deep poverty"—that is, on less than a dollar and twenty-five cents a day. A billion more live on less than two dollars a day. Yet this is not an "exception" to the rule that love casts out fear. Quite the opposite, it is a collective lovelessness on the part of the advanced nations of the world that allows us to accept the reality of deep poverty, thus deflecting a miraculous solution. When we collectively make love our bottom line—making humanitarian values rather than short-term economics the organizing principle of human civilization—then the situation will indeed miraculously change. According to economist Jeffrey Sachs, one hundred billion dollars (one-seventh of the annual military defense budget of the United States) could eradicate deep poverty within ten years.

For those interested in creating the political will to end the worst ravages of hunger and poverty, visit www.results.org. May love prevail among us all.

The Law of
Divine Compensation

CHAPTER I

The Law of Divine Compensation

Some people walk into a room and the word "winner" is written all over them. You don't necessarily know what their secret is, but you wish you had it. Was it their childhood programming? Family connections? Some amazing talent?

As many successful people as there are in the world, there are that many reasons for success. But one kind of material abundance derives from an almost otherworldly charisma, a sense of magic some people carry around with them like an aura of destiny. They may or may not have had the past experiences one normally associates with material success; their success seems almost to have come from something else.

This book is about that "something else" and the power that it gives us. It's about a spiritual zone that has nothing to do with where we've been, how or whether we've been educated, or whether we've succeeded so far or have failed miserably. It's about the ultimate success and perfection of God, potential in all of us whether made manifest or not, yet always available for full expression. Each of us is pregnant with the manifestation of that perfection, for that is who we are.

By aligning yourself with thoughts of infinite love for yourself and others, you gain dominion over the lower thought forms of the world.

This way is not a substitute for any worldly path to success so much as an inner way that informs all others. It is a path to material abundance through immaterial means, and a set of spiritual keys to worldly power. The ways of spirit are not the ways of sacrifice, but rather a way of opening yourself fully to the infinite glories of the universe.

The glories are there. They merely await your acceptance. What follows is an explanation of what they are, how they operate, and how you can tap into them.

The universe is set up to work on your behalf. The world is not a giant, uncaring, random expression of biological processes, but rather a living, breathing reflection of love for all living things. The universe itself is miraculous.

You do not have to believe this, of course. It might not feel that way to you at all.

But spiritual laws aren't called "the good news" for nothing. Spiritual truth is always at work, beyond what the eye can see. It describes an invisible "other world" that exists in a realm beyond our mortal circumstances.

Our interaction with the spiritual world is governed by our thoughts. When we know this truth and consciously align our thoughts with it—sometimes even *despite how we feel*—we activate its spiritual power. We transform our mortal circumstances by bringing our thoughts about them into alignment with a world that lies beyond.

If you think of yourself as being at the effect of a random universe that does not care about you, then you will experience your life that way. If you think of yourself as being at the effect of a loving universe that does care about you, then you will experience your life *that* way.

No matter what is happening in our lives, we choose how we wish to think about it. And the greatest gift we give ourselves is often our willingness to change our minds. Despite what might seem to be the saddest and most intractable situation, we have the power to believe that something else is possible, that things can change, that a miracle can happen.

This simple shift in how we think can make all the difference in what happens next. How we think releases an infinite number of possibilities that could not have occurred *had we not believed that they were possible*. Such is the power of our thoughts to attract as well as deflect miraculous breakthroughs.

Free will means you can think whatever you want to think. You cannot, however, make untrue what is true or true what is untrue. The universe *does* care about you. The universe *is* set up to work on your behalf. And the universe *is* capable of bringing miraculous transformation to any situation of brokenness or lack. Regardless of what has happened in your life, the universe is able and prepared to bring you comfort and repair.

You are loved, and your purpose is to love. From a mind filled with infinite love comes the power to create infinite possibilities. We have the power to think in ways that reflect and attract all the love in the world. Such thinking is called enlightenment. Enlightenment is not a process we work toward, but a choice available to us in any instant.

Enlightenment is the answer to every problem. In any situation where you seem to be at the effect of forces over which you have no control, remember that God dwells within your mind, and there *are* no forces over which He has no control. Therefore, through His power within you, there are no mortal conditions over which you are powerless. Whenever your good is obscured by the appearances of a nonloving world, the universe is programmed to lift you out of that condition and return you to an abundant state.

As an expression of divine perfection, the universe is both self-organizing and self-correcting. To whatever extent your mind is aligned with love, you will receive divine compensation for any lack in your material existence. From spiritual substance will come material manifestation. This is not just a theory; it is a fact. It is a law by which the universe operates. I call it the Law of Divine Compensation.

Just as there are objective, discernible laws of external phenomena, so there are objective, discernible laws of internal phenomena. The law of gravity, for instance, is not just a "belief." It is true whether or not you believe it. Spiritual laws are not just beliefs, either; they are descriptions of how consciousness operates.

Once we know this law—that there is a natural tendency of the universe to improve all things— then we lean naturally into the arms of God and allow Him to lift us up. We surrender our thoughts, then He uplifts our thoughts, then our experiences change.

The practical issue is whether we choose thoughts that activate or deactivate the Law of Divine Compensation. We activate it with every loving thought. We deactivate it when we give more credence to the reality and power of the material world than to the reality and power of love.

If our circumstances tempt us to think thoughts such as, "I must not be good enough," "I will never have another chance," "It will take forever for this to right itself," or "I hate whoever is to blame for this," then miracles, though they are programmed into the nature of the universe, cannot make their way into our awareness. With every thought we think, we either summon or block a miracle.

It is not our circumstances, then, but rather our thoughts about our circumstances, that determine our power to transform them.

The Law of Divine Compensation applies equally to all situations, but in this book we will focus on its application to money and the lack thereof. In a time of economic uncertainty—when circumstances make it particularly tempting to believe in the scarcity of the material plane over the abundance of the spiritual—our capacity to think differently is the miracle-worker's edge.

Bills stare you in the face. Foreclosure looms. Credit is wrecked. Jobs aren't available. And with all that comes chaos on many fronts. Who doesn't need a miracle then?

If you identify only with your body and its reality, rather than with your spirit and *its* reality, then you're tempted to think that diminished material assets somehow diminish who you are. But you are not merely a being of the material world; you are a being of unlimited spirit. *And in spirit there is no lack. You* are not lacking just because your circumstances are.

If your core belief is "I lack" and you carry that belief with you, then you will subconsciously perpetuate or create the circumstances that reflect the belief. But your circumstances are completely malleable: they simply reflect the dictates of your mind.

Regardless of what limits exist in your material world, your immutable truth is that you are an unlimited spiritual being. By remembering this, you summon the Law of Divine Compensation.

You are a loving idea in the Mind of God. Circumstances should not and need not tempt you to believe otherwise. The universe showers you with love not because of what you have done or not done, but because of who you are. Think of the universe itself as a personal love note from God to you. God is love, and in sharing His love you share His power. By aligning yourself with thoughts of infinite love for yourself and others, you gain dominion over the lower thought forms of the world.

In a material sense, your situation might indeed be bleak. You might have been given a raw deal, even been betrayed by others. You yourself might have made a huge mistake. Still, what matters is what you think now: Are you lingering in the past, or are you allowing for a miracle in the present? Are you blaming yourself and others, or blessing yourself and others? Are you clinging to your faith in the reality of the disaster, or opening your mind to the possibility of a miracle? Realign your thoughts with the thoughts of God, and in any given instant the universe is ready to begin again. The laws of time and space are more malleable than we think.

Mistakes and wrong turns need not throw us off. The capacity for correction is built into the universe, just as it is into the workings of a GPS. If you've programmed an address into your GPS but then take a different turn than it recommends, the GPS automatically creates a new route. And so does the universe.

Perhaps you thought you'd get to where you wanted to be financially through achieving a certain credential, doing a particular job, or making a particular investment. But then something happened: the economy worsened, you made a mistake, or someone else did. The Law of Divine Compensation gives us the assurance that the universe will simply create a new route. What is lacking shall become abundant, and what is wounded shall be healed. From "out of the blue"—or miracle-mindedness—miracles will flow forth naturally. Why? Because perfection is your eternal home, to which the universe is programmed to return you whenever you have deviated, for whatever reason, from the thoughts that get and keep you there.

That is how loved you are.

CHAPTER 2

The Power of Faith

Years ago, early in my career as a speaker, I had what I thought was a great idea for an evening of spirituality and musical entertainment. It actually *was* a great idea, but I had another idea that wasn't so great: that instead of telling people how great the evening was going to be, I'd surprise them with it once they got there! Marketing genius, I know. . .

So, of course, not that many people came. After all, I'd promoted it as if you had to just *trust* me that it would be worth your while!

I had rented a huge, beautiful theater; we had fabulous musicians; the evening was really first class and wonderful. Among those who *were* there, a common comment was, "Wow, if I'd known how great this evening was going to be, I would have brought ten friends!" If only.

Faith is not just a theological principle; it is a mental and emotional muscle.

My parents had flown from Houston to Los Angeles for the occasion, and at the end of the show they came backstage to congratulate me. As my father put his arms around me, I burst into tears.

"Oh, Daddy," I sobbed. "It was such a bomb!"

"What are you talking about?" he exclaimed. "It was wonderful!"

"Yeah, but not enough people were here," I complained. "Daddy, I lost *ten thousand* dollars!"

"Aw hell, Little Sister," he said to me. "First of all, I'm proud of you that you've made ten thousand you could lose, and I'm proud of you that you risked it on something so great. If anybody gives you trouble about this, you just tell them *you can absorb the loss.*"

The next day, and for several days thereafter, a girlfriend of mine who was one of the singers in the show kept fretting about my financial loss. But instead of joining in with her dismal, albeit compassionate, outlook, I took my father's advice and kept saying, "Toni, I can absorb the loss." I said it so often I began to convince myself, and in time I think I convinced her, too. I didn't have control at that point over what had happened in the past, but I had control over how I dealt with it now. I had made a mistake, yes, but the universe wouldn't hold me to it. The path toward, or away from, financial recovery lay in how I chose to think about what had happened: as proof of utter failure and doom, or as an opportunity to forgive myself and attract a miracle.

What I needed more than anything right then was *faith*—faith that I could go forward and ultimately recoup my losses.

· · ·

FAITH IS NOT just a theological principle; it is a mental and emotional muscle. It is an aspect of consciousness, a function of the mind. With every attitude we demonstrate faith—either faith in what can go wrong or faith in what can go right. Our problem is that we tend to have tremendous faith in the power of our disasters and far too little faith in the power of miracles.

Our faith itself is a potent force: we increase a thing's power by increasing our *belief* in its power.

Like any muscle, faith grows strong when used and weak when unused. When faith in love and its miraculous authority becomes a thought form that guides our thinking, it turns into an extraordinary power that transforms our lives.

It is not enough that spiritual power exists; we must have *faith* that it exists in order to use it on our behalf. Faith affects our psychological and emotional state, which greatly influences *how* we experience what is happening.

When you're sitting in front of a pile of bills you don't know how you'll pay, or are being hounded by creditors, or are afraid you'll lose your home; when you're confronted by images of economic gloom and doom, recession, and hardship every day, it's easy to fear that your financial state will only get worse. It seems easier to have *faith* in the power of economic loss than to have *faith* in the possibility of economic recovery.

But faith isn't blind; it's visionary. Having faith in a positive outcome doesn't mean you're denying a problem or ignoring obstacles; it simply means you're affirming a solution.

If you believe that economic disaster is the bedrock reality of your existence because your physical senses and mortal circumstances practically scream that it's so, then that belief is a powerful force. Your belief is literally being used against you.

But if you see your current economic hardship as what it *really* is—a temporary deviation from love's perfection, happening within the mortal realm but in ultimate reality not happening at all *because only love is real*—then your vision works a miracle. It frees your energy, thoughts, and emotions, opening your mind to new possibilities.

For that is what a miracle is: a shift in thinking which then shifts your experience. This shift in perception—your willingness to look beyond appearances—enables you to invoke a different set of probabilities going forward. It enables you to see beyond what's happening to what *could* be happening, thus creating the space for something new.

Faith is power. It changes your life by changing *you*. It places you on a different ground of being within yourself. It gives you a confidence based on something that's in you but not of you, that can do for you what you can't do for yourself. It keeps you from sinking into victim consciousness—a stance that attracts more victimization—and lifts you to positivity, which attracts more positive outcomes. Where we put our faith literally and directly influences what happens next.

The Bible's adage "Blessed are those who have faith and cannot see" means "Empowered are those who remember who they are even when circumstances would tempt them to believe otherwise."

It's easy enough to have faith in God's infinite abundance when you have millions of dollars sitting in your bank account, but what's important to remember is that everything seen begins in a place that was first unseen.

When a pilot cannot see the horizon because of low visibility, he or she doesn't assume that the horizon has disappeared. At a time of low visibility, the pilot flies on instruments that can actually gauge a situation more clearly than he can. Faith is like flying on instruments: it's acting on the assumption that just because you can't see a possibility at the moment doesn't mean that it's not there.

And faith is not just knowing that love is always there: faith is also knowing that that which is *not* love is *not* really there! Yes, of course it *is* there within our three-dimensional mortal reality—the bills, the foreclosure, the pink slip, the recession—but that reality is not *ultimate* reality. Your power to invoke ultimate truth lies in your clarity about what is truth and what is illusion. With every thought we think, we display either faith in love or faith in fear.

Faith in love: "I lack a job as the world defines it, but my divine function is established by God. I am here to love and be loved, and that is what establishes my worth. No worldly rejection establishes my value in the universe, and no material lack diminishes my fullness in God. I atone for my errors and forgive others for theirs. I place this situation of apparent lack in His hands and rest in absolute faith that it is miraculously changing *even as I speak this word.*"

Faith in fear: "I am a complete failure. I'm too old to get another job; they're only hiring younger people. The economy won't be picking up for years. All the jobs are taken. The system is rigged. I totally screwed up. I was screwed by so-and-so. I'll never get these bills paid. I'll probably lose my house. I give up. It's no use. It's too late. I blew it. Damn the Democrats. Damn the Republicans. Damn the corporations. Damn the unions. Damn the rich. Damn the poor."

Thoughts placed in the service of fear deactivate the Law of Divine Compensation. Why? Because they are *unloving*. They are attack thoughts, and miracles flow only through the auspices of loving thought. It is love and love alone that gives us the power to transcend the lower thought forms and appearances of the mortal world. Only love of our self and others gives us the divine authority to reset the trajectories by which our life unfolds.

Love's miracles are being created in every given

moment, unobstructed by anything carried over from the past. *That is the way the universe operates.* Your faith in love doesn't determine love's power, but it does determine whether or not you will *experience* that power. You can't turn off the light, but you can put your hands in front of your eyes and then complain that the room is dark. The universe is infinitely and eternally lit with the light of love and new possibility. You can have faith in that and experience miracles. Or you can have faith in the illusions of the mortal world, experiencing lack and scarcity without end.

• • •

I DID RECOUP the ten thousand dollars that I lost so many years ago in Los Angeles, and while I certainly can't say I never made another financial error, I never forgot the lesson my father taught me that night: that I could absorb the loss. Whether through cases where I've made mistakes, or where someone else made mistakes that affected me, I've learned that the products of fear do not permanently stand. Each of us chooses how we will think about what happens in our lives, and to look on a situation with faith in miracles is to look through the eyes and with the power of God.

If you remember that you are a spiritual being, that God alone is the source of your power, and that the universe is inherently designed to provide for your needs, then you are thinking in a miracle-minded way. You are exercising dominion over the mortal plane by remembering that you are not *of* it. You will "just happen" to be seated next to someone who is looking to hire a person with your skill set. You will "just happen" to think up some fabulous new project and effortlessly attain funding. You will "just happen" to receive a check in the mail from someone who has owed you money for years and never repaid you until now.

Why? Because there is a realm of infinite creativity that exists *beyond* the mortal mind, yet *within* the Mind of God. This is not fantasy, but rather the spiritual reality of the universe. If you choose not to believe this, that is your choice; if you choose to believe it, that is your miracle.

The universe is programmed to manifest, through you, the highest possibilities for your creativity and joy. And that never, ever changes. In

God's Mind you are never too old; in God's Mind you are never inadequate; in God's Mind you are not your résumé or your failures. In God's Mind, there is no mistake that you are not given the opportunity to correct, nor anything anyone did to you that cannot be compensated for when you forgive and move on.

Nothing about your material circumstances has the power to stop the engine of cosmic intention that you be blessed. And you are blessed "eternally," which means moment after moment after moment. In any instant, regardless of what has happened in the past, the universe has arranged and is continuing to arrange infinite possibilities for you to prosper. If you cannot see this now—if despair and anxiety hang like a veil before your eyes, preventing you from mustering any faith in God at all—then in this moment lean on mine. One mind joined with another, regardless of their position in time or space, can remove whatever chains would bind us and deliver us to that sweet, sweet realm where things come full circle and there is always a chance to begin again.

CHAPTER 3

Making Love the Bottom Line

To want love, or to believe in the power of love—all that is wonderful. But where the rubber meets the spiritual road is at the place where we decide whether or not to *act* on love.

One place where putting love first is not always easy is in the area of money. This isn't because the issue is more complicated than any other area of life—it's just the entrenched thinking of the world is that profit, not love, is the bottom line. In a world that is dominated by scarcity, that thought makes sense. In a world where scarcity doesn't even exist, it makes no sense at all.

Putting love first isn't a life of "sacrifice," as many have been taught. In fact, it's quite the opposite. Putting love first means knowing who you are and that you're entitled to miracles. Putting love first means knowing that the universe supports you in creating the good, the holy, and the beautiful. It means knowing that you're on the earth for a purpose, and that the purpose itself will create opportunities for its accomplishment.

Putting love first means knowing that the universe supports you in creating the good, the holy, and the beautiful. It means knowing that you're on the earth for a purpose, and that the purpose itself will create opportunities for its accomplishment.

Making love your bottom line doesn't make you "lose"; it's ultimately the way you inevitably gain.

For what you give, you shall receive; and what you withhold will be withheld from you. As a friend of mine once said to me, the universe keeps a perfect set of books.

Making love the bottom line doesn't mean that you have to give everything away or that you'll never charge for your services. The principle of fair exchange gives love to both giver and receiver.

Making love the bottom line doesn't mean that you're compelled to do anything anyone ever asks you to do. Love always gives the loving response—but sometimes the loving response is "no."

But making love the bottom line *does* mean that we take seriously the idea that we are on the earth to do as love would have us do, and to do with our resources only what we are internally guided to do. I know from personal experience that when I've done this, I've gained financially as well as in other ways. And when I have not done this, I've lost.

The path of love might not lead to an immediate, short-term bundle of cash. But following the path of love leads to trust, to deeper relationships, and therefore to a greater probability of further good. Our *internal* abundance is ultimately the source of our *external* abundance. Who we *are,* not just the services we provide, creates money.

People who are positive and energetic when they show up for work—are they or are they not the people most likely to be promoted? People who are kind and helpful when you walk into their store—do they or do they not have a business to which you're more likely to return? People who inspire genuine trust and faith in the excellence of their work—are they or are they not the people you are more likely to hire for your next project? You know that line about how nice guys finish last? It's a lie.

Yet at times we fear that if we give ourselves to love, we will somehow devolve into a puddle of weakness—that love will make us vulnerable to hurt or make us less effective in the world. We think it's okay for God to have our spiritual lives, but we better not hand over our finances! A woman once told me, "I don't mind giving God my money, but if it's over two hundred thousand dollars, I think I better handle it myself." And here is what makes that such a joke: it is often in the area of our finances where we need miracles the most!

Love is our *sanity*. It does not lead us to unwise behavior. It does not lead us to give our money away frivolously when there is a need to save it and provide for our family. It does not lead us to disrespect principles of money management or the appropriate laws of commerce. It does not lead us into unreasonable or immoderate behavior. Love doesn't ruin things; love makes all things right, by aligning mortal events with the natural patterns of an intentional and creative universe.

Love makes us wake up in the morning with a sense of purpose and a flow of creative ideas. Love floods our nervous system with positive energy, making us far more attractive to prospective employers, clients, and creative partners. Love fills us with a powerful charisma, enabling us to produce new ideas and new projects, even within circumstances that seem to be limited. Love leads us to atone for our errors and clean up the mess when we've made mistakes. Love leads us to act with impeccability, integrity, and excellence. Love leads us to serve, to forgive, and to hope. Those things are the opposite of a poverty consciousness; they're the stuff of spiritual wealth creation.

In 1992, I published a book called *A Return to Love*. At the time, I was a bit naive—I had never spent time thinking about things like book contracts, bestseller status, or book royalties. I was happy to be able to live off the suggested donations at my lectures on *A Course in Miracles;* while writing the book I don't think I even thought about how well it might sell. I do remember hoping it would sell enough copies that I wouldn't be embarrassed! In fact, due largely to the enthusiasm of Oprah Winfrey, it was the fifth-bestselling book in America that year.

I had a strong sense at the time that the money hadn't really come directly from the book—that it had come *through* it, but not really *from* it. I felt as if the money was divine payment for something more than the book, particularly the charitable work I had been doing for years before, for no money at all. It was payment for how I had been trying to live my life, cleaning up any mess from my past and trying to be of service to others. The seeker isn't looking to "get money," but to exchange energy. And when the energy we're putting out is filled with the consciousness of love, then the energy flowing back to us comes in whatever form most serves our good. I figured that if I lived a good life and worked hard, I'd be taken care of somehow.

There was a level of naiveté to the life I was living before that book was published. I had never transitioned to the more sophisticated principles by which wealth is supposedly created, and as a consequence I was blessedly unaware of them. There's no way in the world that my activities during those years would have been thought to be good for business, because there *was* no business! But I was, in my own way, "about my Father's business." And then, when the book was published, I saw that what I had done for love came back to me a thousandfold and more.

Such is the Law.

CHAPTER 4

Transforming a Negative Sense of Self

The Law of Divine Compensation represents the natural working of the universe, but it's up to each of us to rid our minds of the thoughts that block it. Unloving thoughts deactivate the Law. They sabotage the dynamic by which the universe is programmed to support us.

When we think or say something negative, even if we believe we don't really mean it, the thought carries creative energy. Every thought is a cause that creates an effect. An undisciplined mind, easily tempted into faithless and unloving thoughts, is a huge deterrent to success.

Negative thoughts that deactivate the Law of Divine Compensation tend to fall into three major categories: (1) negative sense of self, (2) anger, and (3) guilt. We'll look at these categories in this and the next two chapters, starting with a negative sense of self.

Spiritual growth involves giving up the stories of your past so the universe can write a new one.

Releasing negative self-concepts is important not simply because they hurt you; it's important because *they're not true*. The spiritual journey is a path of surrendering our fear-based thoughts and allowing them to be replaced by God's. The reason to embrace a positive self-image is that it describes you as God thinks of you.

Contrary to the thoughts of God, however, are the numerous negative self-images we allow to freely wander through our minds:

"I'm not good enough."

"I'm a loser."

"I don't have what it takes."

"My father [or mother, or teacher, etc.] was right about me. I will never amount to anything."

"I'm dumb."

"I'm a failure."

"I don't have enough talent."

"I'm too old."

"Nobody wants me."

"Nobody appreciates me."

"I'm a has-been."

"All the good jobs have been sent overseas."

"There's no job out there for me."

"It does no good to even try at this point."

"I've been screwed over."

"The system is f***ed."

Such painful thoughts arise from over-identification with the material plane. Identifying with your material self rather than with your spiritual self will always leave you vulnerable to self-hating projections, because the mortal self is not who you are. The mortal plane is, at best, an ever-changing parade of individual perceptions that lack a consistent theme. Sometimes you'll deem yourself worthy of self-regard, and sometimes you won't—depending on what's in your bank account, other people's opinions of you, and so forth. Hardly a great basis for career success . . .

On the mortal plane, none of us are perfect all the time. But on the spiritual plane, all of us are perfect all the time. Who we *really* are—perfect creations of God, unchangeable and unlimited, none of us more or less brilliant than anyone else—is the most positive self-concept possible. To self-identify according to your spiritual rather than material reality is enlightenment. From this perspective, you see that you *are* the light. No thought or condition of darkness—that is, lovelessness in your own mind or in anyone else's—has any bearing whatsoever on the truth of who you are or what the universe has planned for you. Your past, your mistakes, other people's opinions about you, even your failures do not in any way limit who you are or what is possible for you now.

ONE OF THE most common negative self-concepts we carry—one that underlies many other wrong-minded sentiments—is that we're simply not good enough; that something about us is defective.

It can be tempting to believe that "some of us have it, and some of us don't." Some of us are talented, while others of us aren't. Some of us are brilliant, while others of us aren't. Some of us are born to succeed, while others of us aren't. And we often see ourselves in the latter half of those comparisons.

As long as we think we're separate from the rest of the universe, we're bound to compare ourselves to others.

A Course in Miracles teaches us that all of us are special and none of us are special. All of us carry the mark of God, yet we carry that mark as one. No one has any more or less capacity than anyone else to be used as a conduit for the genius that pours forth constantly from the Mind of God. This genius pours into us as one, but is accepted by us separately. God's greatness is a gift that is offered to all of us, but it's our choice whether or not to receive it.

We lack faith in *what* exists within us because we lack faith in *Who* exists within us.

Each of us has a unique part to play in the healing of the world. Each of us is assigned by God a
function that only we can fill. At the level of our
divine function, none of us are in competition with
each other, for the universe has an infinite number
of pieces of pie. My piece doesn't take away from
yours, and yours doesn't take away from mine.
There is space for *everyone's* gifts to flower. There is
more than enough room for all of us.

When futurist and universally acknowledged
genius Buckminster Fuller was asked his definition
of a genius, his response was, "Someone who had
the right mother." I assume he meant someone who
had the most positive childhood programming,
someone who was told when young that he or she
was brilliant and *would* succeed. If told as children
that we're bound to succeed, then we tend to. If
told as children that we're bound to fail, then we
tend to do that instead.

But even if your mother or father didn't tell you
that you were wonderful when you were a child,
your divine Father/Mother tells you that now.
Spiritual understanding is a corrective to any false
programming you might have received as a child.

Rather than endlessly analyzing a tape from child-hood, you can erase it by recording a new one. A story, no matter how factually true, is still just a story. Spiritual growth involves giving up the stories of your past so the universe can write a new one. You are not denying your childhood; you are simply transcending any of its negative aspects.

You are a child of God, carrying the eternal mark of your perfect Source. You are naturally entitled to miracles because love is what you are. This is not an arrogant appraisal of the ego, but rather a humble acceptance of God's truth. You just happen to have within you the eternal power of the universe.

Because you are a child of God, made of love, only love has power over you. Your mortal self can be damaged, but your spiritual self cannot. You do not have to identify with the brokenness of the world, for the effects of brokenness are temporary. *Every loving thing that ever happened to you was real, and everything else was an illusion.* Such illusions have no effect on your future unless you carry them with you into the present. It is entirely up to each of us whether we consider ourselves damaged goods.

Of course things might have gone roughly in the past, but the past is over and cannot touch you unless you hold on to it. Right now, in this moment, the universe is responding not to your past but to the truth of who you are, always were, and always will be.

We've all got the "right stuff" because all of us are hosts to God; His voice, and not the fear-based ego's, is the voice we can listen to and learn to follow. Each of us is meant to channel the spiritual realities of talent, creativity, and intelligence. This is nothing to take personal credit for, but nothing to apologize for either. As a child of God, you just *happen* to be the recipient of endless power and possibility. Whether or not you've always known this, or practiced it, there lies within you in this very moment the latent ability to create and achieve beyond your wildest dreams.

And this never changes. No mortal condition diminishes the power of God. It doesn't matter what your résumé is, or how many degrees you have. It doesn't matter what mistakes you've made, or how the economy is doing. It matters only where you place your consciousness now. Know who you are and Who lives within you, and moving mountains will seem small compared to what you can do.

THIS RECOGNITION OF God's infinite power, and infinite love for us, is important in relation to another negative self-concept that weighs heavily on many people: the thought that we're too old to manifest work or money.

Once again, we are challenged to think as God thinks. The body ages, but the spirit does not. Never at any point does the universe give up on us, consider us not good enough, or consider us has-beens. Only if you think of *yourself* in such ways can you block the flow of miracles to your door.

Women particularly are tempted to believe that our value declines with our physical beauty. Yet sometimes it's when our outer beauty begins to fade that our inner beauty shines most brightly. In the words of Ralph Waldo Emerson, "As we grow old, the beauty steals inward." To the universe, we are never invisible.

It's true that in youth we have some wonderful things that we lose when we're older, but it's also true that when we're older we have some wonderful things we didn't have when we were young. The gifts of age aren't quite as tangible as the gifts of youth, but they are no less real. As we claim them—fully appreciating the nonmaterial gift of wisdom that comes from accumulated life experience—the universe will follow our lead, reflecting back to us the value we first accorded to ourselves. As Emily Dickinson wrote, "We turn not older with years, but newer every day."

Yes, if you're older, there might be people who won't want to hire you because of it; but the miraculous universe doesn't care about that. The universe is flexible, and if we're open to infinite possibilities, then possibilities will appear. According to *A Course in Miracles,* "Miracles are natural. When they do not occur, something has gone wrong." There are examples in the world today of hot and happening octogenarians! If Betty White can be the hottest mama in Cleveland, then surely anything is possible. I don't think anyone believes that *she* can't find work.

So how do we quit the negative self-talk, the chronic repetition of thoughts and feelings that cause us to emotionally spiral downward? It's not always as easy as simply saying, "I won't think that way anymore." Entrenched thought forms are like a buildup of plaque on our consciousness. But we're not asked to be our own transformers; we're asked only to surrender the thoughts and feelings that need transforming.

According to *A Course in Miracles*, "Through prayer love is received, and through miracles love is expressed."

> *Dear God,*
>
> *I feel myself falling into the hole of self-pity, self-obsession, and negativity.*
>
> *I know I shouldn't think this way, but I'm afraid and I cannot stop.*
>
> *Please replace my thoughts with Yours, dear God.*
>
> *I am willing to see myself and all things differently.*
>
> *Please send me the miracle of new eyes and ears, that*
> *I might know my greater good.*
>
> *Amen.*

CHAPTER 5

Releasing Anger

Anger is a second category of thoughts that deactivate the power of the Law of Divine Compensation. Anger is an emotional impurity that hardens the heart and closes the mind.

I am not denying that there are many understandable reasons why we get angry. Perhaps you find yourself in debt, underemployed, or unemployed through no fault of your own. Someone may have unfairly fired you, lied about you to a superior, stolen money from you, or exploited you for financial gain. Despite trying to be as responsible as possible, you were simply swept aside by circumstances beyond your control.

Those things do happen. And it is natural to feel angry when they do.

Even then, however, love is the answer. Without love, the universe cannot program itself to compensate for whatever might have been taken from us. If we do not let go of our anger, it can block the miraculous universe, empowering the idea that we were victimized and then recreating the scenario in which we are.

We forgive, then, out of self-interest. I forgive you because I want out of my pain. I forgive you so that I can be free of what you did. I see beyond your mistake to the love in you so that I can see beyond the mistake to the love in me—because only then can I have a miracle.

We were not created to be at the effect of love-lessness either in ourselves or in others. As it says in *A Course in Miracles,* "The Christ in you cannot be crucified." The material self can be wronged, but the spiritual self cannot be. Feel your feelings, yes, but be self-aware enough to know the difference between processing and spewing. Feeling your feelings is healthy; holding on to them longer than you need to is self-indulgent. Express your anger in a safe environment, and then know when it's time to stop verbalizing your pain.

It doesn't matter if someone tells you that you "deserve" to be angry—you *deserve,* of course, to feel whatever you want to feel! But the only way to experience miracles is to think about situations in a miracle-minded way. Holding on to anger hurts no one but yourself. As it says in *A Course in Miracles,* "Do you prefer to be right or to be happy?" Is your goal to summon co-complainers who join with you in the thought that you were victimized, or would you prefer spiritual companions who join you in knowing that as a child of God you can't *be* victimized?

The universe knows if you were hurt and is already on the case to make right whatever wrong occurred. Your anger, if it lingers, throws a wrench in the machine of the miraculous universe.

Let's say your financial good was blocked by someone, or by forces outside your control. You were not necessarily the *cause* of what happened to you, but you are responsible for how you contextualize it. Yes, whatever happened, happened; but what happens *now* is up to you. You can respond from ego, ensuring pain; or you can respond from spirit, ensuring a miracle.

The level of woundedness is the level of illusion. By identifying with this level, we experience effects at this level. Something has the power to hurt us to the extent to which we believe in its power. If we believe in the reality of a wound, then we will feel really wounded. The healing lies in remembering what is real.

Lovelessness is not ultimately real. It exists within a three-dimensional reality, but you are more than merely a being of the mortal plane. In remembering this, you rise above the chronic suffering that plagues this world. You are lifted into the immortal realms, where anything that isn't love falls away from you naturally, and you suffer no more.

Will this take time to express itself? Yes, perhaps. But how quickly your thinking changes helps determine how quickly your mortal circumstances change.

This doesn't mean we're foolishly denying that something bad occurred; we're simply denying its power to ultimately affect us. Anger, if it exists, must be acknowledged by all means, but acting on it dysfunctionally is precarious at best and destructive at worst. We should feel our anger, accept that it is there, and then surrender it to the Holy Spirit for transformation. Then, instead of putting our energy into deriding what is, we become capable of affirming and creating what could be. Something miraculous happens when we say, "I am angry but I am willing not to be. Dear God, help me see this situation differently. Amen."

Sometimes we're angry with people we don't even know. Many feel understandable anger at banks, politicians, Wall Street, and all those who have grown rich—or served only the rich—at everyone else's expense. There is legitimate moral outrage regarding today's economic environment. But moral outrage does not have to include personal anger.

Martin Luther King Jr. was outraged by legalized segregation, but his nonviolent temperament lifted him above personal anger. Mahatma Gandhi was outraged by the British colonization of India, but his nonviolent temperament lifted him above personal anger. Notice how in both cases, the fact that these men were lifted above the lower energy of anger empowered them to be even more effective at eradicating the conditions that outraged them. Nonviolence didn't mean they looked *away* from the problem; it meant they looked *through* it to a realm of possibility that lay beyond the conditions that angered them. That ability—the miracle-worker's spiritual authority, if you will—gave them the power to invoke the world they wished to see.

By holding on to my anger, I am attaching myself to the realm in which I can *be* made angry. I am seeing someone outside myself as the source of my loss, thus dooming myself to experience the loss. In a perverse way, it's as though I am idolizing the very people who hurt me. For if I'm thinking they can take away my good, then I must be thinking they were the *source* of my good! I must be thinking they're more powerful than God, since

I'm thinking they can permanently remove from me what God wills me to have.

BEYOND OUR ANGER lies our capacity to forgive. Forgiveness is looking at people with the spiritual knowledge of their innocence rather than the mortal perception of their guilt.

Forgiveness is indeed a different way of thinking, in that it surrenders the very aspect of mind that we think protects us from further hurt. But the ego's "protection" is precarious, at best. I don't "protect" myself when I lash out in anger. Forgiveness is a radical act, but it is certainly not weakness. By forgiving, we do not grant victory to those who wronged us; instead, we surrender the aspect of mind that is blocking divine correction. *Not* forgiving, then, is granting victory to those who wronged us, in that we allow them to shape our reality. Anger, defensiveness, martyrdom, and so forth do not attract miracles. Mercy and compassion do.

To place a problem into the hands of God is to pray that our *thinking* about the problem be changed. If only love is real, and only love has dominion over us, then our mistakes and the mistakes of others can affect us only if we choose to hold on to them.

We forgive, then, out of self-interest. I forgive you because I want out of my pain. I forgive you so that I can be free of what you did. I see beyond your mistake to the love in you so that I can see beyond the mistake to the love in me—because only then can I have a miracle. The universe will immediately reprogram itself to send us miracles, when we remove the barriers to our willingness to love. Forgiveness is the most powerful key to new beginnings.

None of this is always easy. It's hard when thirty years of your hard work is thrown to the side in a cold, calculating business decision made by someone half your age. It's painful when someone you've trusted steals your money, lies about you, or throws you under the bus. But anger and condemnation will only delay the healing. As hard as it might be at times to summon up the willingness to love, *A Course in Miracles* says that our "little willingness is everything." When we're willing to see the innocence in another person even when he or she has behaved without love toward us, we activate the Law of Divine Compensation.

Then the flow of miracles automatically begins. The flow will come in whatever form best compensates for the original error, including—if that will serve you best—far more money than you originally lost.

Should you seek legal redress for any harm you were caused, if indeed that was the case? Perhaps, if that's what you internally feel guided to do. But unless you seek to forgive as well, no amount of money will heal your pain. No matter how much worldly justice you're accorded, you'll still feel a wound to your heart. External justice will do us little good if we remain internally victimized.

It may be, in fact, that the most loving thing we can do is to redress a wrong done at our expense or at the expense of someone else. Committing ourselves to a path of love does not mean we ignore the importance of justice. We must always act for justice, because justice is of God. But we seek to let go of the internal tension that blocks the flow of love.

It's often said that we can be bitter or we can be better. If we carry anger and blame forward, we will inevitably become bitter. Bitterness is hardly the personality trait that someone out there is looking to hire, partner with, promote, or invest in. Our clinging to old wounds might inspire sympathy for a time, or even temporary support. But it will not inspire invitations to start over, from other people or from the universe itself.

> *Dear God,*
>
> *Please help me to forgive my mistakes of the past.*
>
> *Please help me to forgive those who denied me my good.*
>
> *Please show me the innocence inside us all.*
>
> *I am willing to see that only love is real,*
>
> *But the pain of circumstances holds a grip on my heart.*
>
> *Please flood my mind with divine perception,*
>
> *That I might see through the veil of illusion*
>
> *And be free to begin again.*
>
> *Thank you, God.*
>
> *Amen.*

CHAPTER 6

Beyond Guilt

Another major category of thoughts that deactivate the Law of Divine Compensation is guilt.

Sometimes we have a pretty good success rate at forgiving others, but we aren't so good at forgiving ourselves. We think, "Okay, I can believe that the universe was programmed to give me what would make me happy, but then I *blew* it. And I can't forgive myself."

Many of us have some unpleasant and even painful memories tied up with money, and a lot of them fall under the category of "my own damn fault."

Given the significant impact that financial errors can have on our lives and the lives of our families, the feelings of guilt can be terrible. If one of our children can't have dance classes this year because of a mistake we made, or can't go to college or have the wedding of her dreams—and sometimes the consequences are far worse—then the feelings of failure can be intense.

We may have made mistakes in our past, but we're not bound by those mistakes in the present— as long as we're willing to think now as we did not think then, act now as we did not act then, clean up in the present what needs to be cleaned up from the past, and be now who we were not then.

The ego is that which both sets you up to do the wrong thing and then punishes you viciously for having done so. It lures you into doing something stupid, and then would have you believe that you're the dumbest, most irresponsible human being alive for having made such a mistake! Now, it argues, everything is terrible and will only be getting worse!

Yet the ego lies. It lied when it convinced you to do something stupid; and it also lies when it tells you that you're a terrible person for whom there is no hope, now that you've done such a terrible thing.

Guilt is savage, and it never lets you off the hook. It leads to obsession, self-hatred, self-punishment, and a shattered sense of self.

Yet we must always remember: guilt is untrue, for you were created as an innocent child of God, and His reality is changeless. That is why it is built into the nature of the universe that you can compensate for past errors and begin again.

SOMETIMES WHEN WE'VE made a mistake, well-meaning people will try to console us by saying things like, "It happened for a reason," when we know in our hearts, "Yes, it happened for a reason, and I'll tell you what it was: *I made a dumb mistake!*" Sometimes we need to face the harsh reality that we *did* make a mistake, and look at the fact with open eyes.

This quote from the *I Ching* speaks powerfully to our need for brutal self-honesty when we have made mistakes: "It is only when we have the courage to face things exactly as they are, without any self-deception or illusion, that a light will develop out of events, by which the path to success may be recognized."

We might need to feel the shame of knowing that we did something stupid, and burn through the pain of that, but we'll come out on the other side of it a more humble person, with greater integrity and groundedness. A failure remains a failure only if we refuse to learn from it. Any situation that teaches us greater humility, sobriety, wisdom about self and others, responsibility, forgiveness, depth of reflection, and better decision-making—teaching us what's truly important—is not an ultimate failure. Sometimes what we deem a failure at the time it happens actually serves to foster a change within us that creates an even greater success down the road.

Great people are not those who have never fallen

down. Great people are those who, when they do fall down, dig deep within themselves and find the strength to get back up. Sometimes that dark night of the soul teaches us some very important things about ourselves—about who we've been, and who we choose to be now; about where we got it right, and where we got it wrong. Spiritually healthy people are those who take responsibility for their mistakes, atone for their errors, do what they can to make things right, and allow forgiveness and mercy to wash them clean.

If you're like the rest of us, of course you've screwed up royally at one point or another. But it doesn't serve you, or anyone else, for you to beat up on yourself continually. Have appropriate remorse? Yes. Grow from your mistakes and make things right as best you can? Yes. But stay stuck in the mire of self-hatred? Absolutely not. We may have made mistakes in our past, but we're not bound by those mistakes in the present—as long as we're willing to think now as we did not think then, act now as we did not act then, clean up in the present what needs to be cleaned up from the past, and be now who we were not then.

· · ·

WHEN WE TAKE full responsibility for the places where we know in our hearts we underperformed in the past, or acted without integrity, or failed to respect opportunities and abundance that once were ours, we experience the miracle of the Atonement. Atonement is a mental process through which we correct our perceptions, thus changing the trajectory of probabilities that unfold as a result.

Atonement is like a spiritual reset button. It is a gift from God, providing us the opportunity to clear the karma of past mistakes by owning them, taking responsibility for them, admitting them, making amends for them, and doing whatever is possible to change the patterns of behavior that created the situation that now causes us shame.

We recognize past errors and pray, "I am willing to be different than I was before. Please show me how." The universe then corrects all limitations caused by our wrong-minded thinking. Guilt dissolves from our mind as thoughts of mercy and love replace it.

Buddha described the Law of Karma, or Cause and Effect: for every action there is a reaction.

Therefore, if we acted without wisdom, suffering is to be expected. Jesus, some five hundred years later, revealed the alchemy of God's mercy, which posits that in a moment of grace, all karma is burned, and all debts are paid and forgiven. From Catholics at confession, to Jews on the Day of Atonement, to people taking their moral inventory at a twelve-step meeting, the notion of the Atonement is part of the wisdom teachings of all the major religious and spiritual systems of the world.

Atonement can bring a profound level of humbling—as we sit before piles of credit card bills and face the uncomfortable realization that we should have been more responsible, or we think back on what got us fired and know in our hearts that we ourselves were the problem. Perhaps we played into the drunken maelstrom of financial headiness that characterized the last few decades in our society. Perhaps we bought too much, saved too little, or were otherwise cavalier about money or frivolous in how we dealt with it. Atonement gives us the power to forgive ourselves; it gives us back our self-respect. We've done whatever we could to right our wrongs, and the tenderness of a merciful universe opens up for us in ways we might never have imagined.

There is no mistake you've ever made that can't be divinely corrected, as long as you acknowledge whatever mistaken thoughts led to the error and surrender them to God.

In *A Course in Miracles,* we're told to go back to the moment when the error occurred, admit that we didn't allow God's spirit to guide our decision at the time, but remember that we can choose again *now.* And that is what we do: we place that moment in the hands of God and know that we need not feel guilty, because "He will undo all consequences of our wrong decision if we will let Him."

Miracles transcend the laws of time and space. In the miraculous present, mistakes of the past are undone.

The time it takes for the material world to reflect our shift from fear-based to miracle-minded thinking is symbolized in the Old Testament by the forty years it took for the Israelites, after fleeing their slave condition, to reach the Promised Land. It is expressed in the New Testament by the three days after the crucifixion before Jesus rose. In the biblical stories of both Moses and Jesus, the mind of one close to God became a conduit for the reconstruction of the mortal world. We, too, through the power of our thinking, can radically shift our experience of the world.

God loves us the same when we do the wise thing as when we make mistakes. His love for us is based not on our behavior but on who we are, and He knows who we are—innocent within—because He made us that way. When we make a mistake, it's because in the moment we make it we *forget* who we are, and His response to that is not to punish us but to correct us.

This doesn't mean you don't have to do anything to make things right; in fact, any lesson you might have failed to learn before, you will have to learn now. The mercy of the universe lies in the fact that you are given the opportunity to do that. You might not get a bigger paycheck right away; you might have to humble yourself and make do with less for a while. You might not be Mr. or Ms. Big Shot in a new position; you might have to be brought down a few notches before you can make your next big move up. But you will see the handwriting of God in all of it, if you participate in—rather than resist—the balancing of the spiritual scales. You will know in your heart that this is a good thing, and you will be glad to earn your way back into the abundant realm. Once you have reclaimed your *inner* prosperity, the universe will begin the process of reclaiming it *externally*.

You are internally programmed to rise to your highest creative possibility. Nothing you do can erase the yearning of your soul to achieve it, or the yearning of the universe to give it to you. No deviation from love—on your part or anyone else's—can keep the universe from its divine intention that your life be one of fullness and joy.

According to *A Course in Miracles,* any miracle you might have deflected is "held in trust for you until you are ready to receive it." The universe has an inbuilt insurance policy. Whatever you have lost is programmed to return—in another form, in another situation, in another town, or with other people, perhaps, but through the power of atonement, it *will* return.

Dear God,

I feel that I have failed.

I feel that all my efforts have come to naught.

I feel shame at the way my life has turned out.

I do not know what to do or where to go.

Please, dear God, repair my heart,

Heal my mind, and change my life.

Pave a way for me out of darkness into light.

I atone for my errors, and I pray for forgiveness.

Please do for me what I cannot do.

Thank you, God.

Amen.

CHAPTER 7

Facing Our Prejudice

Another way we deflect wealth is through the unrecognizable belief that it's not really *okay* to have money. Just as some people are prejudiced against the poor, some are prejudiced against the rich.

I support the Occupy Wall Street movement, because over the last few decades there has been a systematic dismantling of the appropriate guarantees of economic justice in the United States. But I noticed, among a few of the Occupiers I met, that their passion seemed to be less an enthusiasm for the rights of all people to participate in the engine of economic prosperity and more a knee-jerk criticism of anyone who does. This then leaves the movement open to all kinds of erroneous criticism—that supporters of Occupy are anti-rich, and so forth. That's hardly the case. The message isn't that people shouldn't be able to get rich in America; it's that the playing field should be so level that with enough hard work *anyone* can! And money should be able to buy a lot of things in America; it just shouldn't be able to buy our government.

**As long as we're making money
righteously, we're not only
receiving a blessing
but also extending one to others.**

No matter how much we struggle for financial abundance, we'll have a hard time attaining it if we disapprove of those who have it. If we're saying one thing but thinking another, we'll always end up with confused results. Many people set themselves up to lose, working hard yet giving an ambivalent message to the universe about whether or not they really want money.

Thoughts like "I want it, but I *shouldn't* want it, so I guess no, I don't really want it; but actually I do want it, but I don't want to admit that I want it" indicate ambivalence. This confusing mix of thoughts inevitably brings forth a confusing mix of experiences. Many people fail to manifest money because on some deep level they don't think they should.

Having been taught that poverty is holy, perhaps they think that rich people are therefore not holy. Having been taught that wealth is a finite resource, some people think that to manifest money for themselves is, by definition, to take money away from someone else. Whatever their reason is, many people don't think it's okay to desire money. And if you disown the desire, you literally disown the money.

THIS BOOK DEALS not only with how we attract miracles, but also with how we deflect them. Judgment is one of the biggest barriers to our own miraculous breakthroughs. If we judge someone else for having wealth, then we'll subconsciously sabotage our own. If we have the idea that somehow it's more *pure* to be poor, then that's most probably what we'll manifest.

I once received a letter from a woman named Judy, who ran a business called Café Joy. She told me she was despondent because her café was getting ready to close. She owed her landlord money, and a neighboring business was making an unfair play for her space. She wrote:

> We've been working hard for four years to keep this place going. This place is so special, and I would be devastated to lose it all. Not only do we serve healthy food, but we created what many people say is a beautiful, peaceful place. We also created a community and supported and brought together artists, as well as neighbors and colleagues, . . . becoming a very special, important place to people in our neighborhood. It was never a venture for money—the importance was always on fellowship and good health—so I'm feeling sad

and confused about why it's being taken from us . . . and especially upset to lose the space to people who are simply able to pay more.

When Judy and I spoke, I loved her passion and vision for the café, but I also noticed that she had some interesting attitudes about money, business, and capitalism in general. As a business owner, she needed to make a profit in order to stay afloat, yet she said things that made it clear she didn't respect the effort to do so. She spoke of profit with a subtle disdain. Whether she wanted to admit it or not, as an operator of a small business she *was* a capitalist; yet she also seemed to project onto all capitalist ventures that they're an unethical rip-off of the 99 percent!

Judy was giving mixed messages to the universe, her conscious mind *saying* one thing and her sub-conscious *hearing* another. In talking to her further, I learned that she had both a degree in social work and a background in the nonprofit world, as well as excellent business skills. Integrated, her past experiences could have been a marvelous marriage of values and material aptitude. But those things were at war with each other inside her. Judy was operating in conflict with herself: she was a business owner, yes, but it was almost as though she was *ashamed* of the fact. It was like she didn't want to admit to herself that the business had to make money in order to survive, because somehow that would make the venture unholy or impure.

Judy's challenge was to make peace with the fact that her café required a profit. And she could do that only by looking more deeply at why she'd ever thought it shouldn't.

"I've never wanted to have more than the next person," she told me, as though her having more than other people somehow made less abundance available to them. This picture of the financial world, in which we assume that there are only so many pieces of the pie and if I have a slice then there's less available to you, is called a *zero-sum game*. If I feel that by asking you to pay me I'm ripping you off, of course I'll feel guilty about charging you money! This will then confuse the universal programming and deflect my abundance.

But if I feel that I'm providing an honorable service, asking for an equitable and fair pay in return, then I can feel good about the exchange *because I'm increasing abundance for both of us.* Fair exchange is a spiritual, not just an economic, principle. As long as we're making money righteously, we're not only receiving a blessing but also extending one to others.

The spiritual universe does *not* operate as a zero-sum game. In the realm of spirit there is infinite abundance, and my creativity does not take from yours; in fact, it adds to yours. I provide energy through a service or product, and you provide energy through the money you pay for it. With an equitable exchange, both parties profit.

Judy told me she'd prayed to be released from any resistance she had to making money, and during our conversation we looked deeply at where the resistance came from. Deeply embedded core beliefs, when they cause a problem, aren't magically removed for us when we pray that the problem be solved. Such beliefs are *brought to consciousness* when we pray; then it's our responsibility to surrender them and *ask* that they be removed. The Holy Spirit will take from us only what we're willing to release.

Judy mentioned that she had a habit of saying to her customers—*she even had it written on the menu!*—the words, "Thank you for your support." I tilted my head when I heard that, asking, "Why wouldn't you say, 'Thank you for your business'?"

She began to recognize what her resistance was—namely, her unrecognized belief that there was something unfair or unrighteous about making money. On one hand, she needed to make money in order for the business to thrive, and she was well aware that she and those she employed worked very hard and provided a beautiful service to the community. On the other hand, she had ambivalent feelings about receiving money. The war raged within her, and so it raged at her café.

Once again, everything we experience in the world is a reflection of our thoughts. If you feel ashamed about celebrating money, don't expect money to celebrate you. If your making money is a rip-off of others, an exploitation or unfair reach into someone else's pocket, then as a righteous person you *won't* feel good about it, nor should you.

But Judy's café is what free-market capitalism should be. There is nothing there to be *ashamed* of. (Many people don't realize that capitalism has different faces in different industrialized societies. A critique of unethical business practices is *not* an inherent critique of capitalism itself.)

I asked Judy why she felt the need to hold her clientele in such a pitiful light—as though they were orphans in *Oliver Twist* rather than abundant adults. Was that really doing them a service, almost infantilizing them in the name of economic fairness? As a social worker, Judy had come in contact with many people who were down and out and needed a helping hand; perhaps she had brought into her work as a café owner an energy that had been appropriate in her social work but was not necessarily appropriate here. Her customers weren't coming to her for help; *they were coming to her for coffee!*

The Law of Divine Compensation would bring about every miracle she needed: a way to settle righteously with her landlord, as well as a way to reopen Café Joy. What Judy needed more than anything was to align her thinking with the natural patterns of the universe, and for that we prayed. She adopted a different attitude and opened herself to new beginnings.

I've heard it said that prayer doesn't change a situation for you so much as it changes you for the situation. It changes the effects in your life because it changes you on the level of cause. Heisenberg's Uncertainty Principle states that when the perceiver changes, that which is perceived then changes. The fact that Judy achieved a new attitude meant—*literally,* not just figuratively—that opportunities she would not otherwise have experienced would now appear.

If she'd stayed in "Ain't it awful," "I hate my landlord," "Damn the owner of the business next door," and "There's no hope now," simply adding the event to her "victim résumé," the universe would absolutely have proved her right. If we convince ourselves that there is no hope, our subconscious mind edits out of the picture any evidence that might prove otherwise.

Hopelessness and negativity could have led to many different things for Judy, none of them miraculous: depression, anxiety, bitterness, resentment, anger, an attitude of victimization, and many other forms of suffering. The landlord had been a jerk, after all; the neighbor had been unethical; and the customers at the old café had taken advantage of her. There were many places where she could have tarried, had she chosen; fear has many addresses.

But Judy wanted a miracle, and she was ready to receive one. In *A Course in Miracles*, it says that we can have a grievance or we can have a miracle; we cannot have both. Judy's job was to heal her mind, no matter how difficult that task was, of false beliefs, anger, and resentment—and to remember, as it says in *A Course in Miracles*, that "there is no order of difficulty in miracles." Those things she did assiduously. She looked at the mistakes she had made in the past, she was open to correcting them, and she was ready to move forward from a higher state of mind.

Another thing Judy was being asked to give up was her attachment to form. She had always been attached to the *particular* neighborhood and the *particular* physical space of her old café. But the universe will never support us in an attachment to form. Often we say, "I want my good to come in this specific way"—*this* money, *that* job, *this* place to live, *that* person, and so forth. But love is not form; it is content. God's promise is not that we will always get what we want. It's that in all things love will ultimately prevail.

As a reflection of the Mind of God, the universe *intends* that you self-actualize, and sometimes that means *not* getting what you want in order to realize that you're fine without it—which counterintuitively then paves the way for you to attract that or something better!

The universe was invested not in Judy's café, but in Judy's enlightenment. Self-actualization involves *detachment,* not *attachment* to form; it acknowledges that form is limited, but spirit is not. And that is why we let go: we release our attachment to form so that universal substance can rearrange it. We pray, "Dear God, I surrender. I've tried to control this situation— I've worked as hard as I can—and now everything has fallen apart. All I have left is to pray for a miracle. Please guide my thinking to a higher place. Amen." Spiritually, that's not the end, but the beginning.

It's almost amusing when doctors say, "We've done everything possible. All we can do now is pray," as though God were simply our last resort, the one we go to when all the *really* powerful things have failed. After all, what's the infinite power of the universe compared to our science and technology and so forth?

We activate our spiritual power by praying from the first moment that an idea presents itself:

> *Dear God,*
>
> *May this business idea be of service to the greater good of all.*
>
> *If it is not the best use of my talents, please cast it from my mind.*
>
> *If it is the best use of my talents, please pave the way for its success.*
>
> *Guide all my thinking and my actions.*
>
> *Amen.*

Pray each day that your work be of service to the healing of the world:

> *Dear God,*
>
> *May this business be a blessing on everyone who works here and everyone it serves.*
>
> *May it both bring and attract prosperity and love.*
>
> *Amen.*

Remember: You are not asking that a force outside of you magically change external circumstances; you are asking that a Divine Guide *within* you change the nature of your thoughts. And when something in your business goes wrong? Say this:

Dear God,

I know that You are bigger than my business problem, but by myself I cannot fix this.

Please guide my thinking, open my heart, and send me a miracle.

Amen.

Before Judy left my apartment that day, we walked out onto the balcony and looked at the view of the city below. Looking into the distance, we could see where her café was, but we could also see other streets and other neighborhoods. The point was obvious: God is not bound by form.

Then changes began to happen as the shifts in her thinking bore fruit. It wasn't too long before Judy found a perfect new location for her café. She was able to make a decent settlement with her old landlord; a relative impressed by her hard work and positive attitude provided financing for her move into the new place; and other forms of support came "out of the blue." All of this brought energy back to her personality, a smile back to her face, and form back to her beloved idea of a café that was in service to its community. Judy's internal abundance—her willingness to work hard, her integrity, her love of her mission, her vigilance about her own thinking, and her faith—invoked the Law of Divine Compensation. What once appeared to be a lack in her life turned into an even greater good.

Our circumstances can shift, and they often do, but God's love is fixed and unalterable. Love's compensatory response to lack or limitation of any kind is built into the patterns of the universe. No matter what our problem is, the universe is *on it*. Judy absorbed her loss; or more specifically, the Holy Spirit absorbed it for her.

CHAPTER 8

Spiritual Surrender

No one likes to worry about money. No one likes to lose their job. No one wants to face the possibility of being broke. But these things happen. And, when they do, they're not random incidents.

The Law of Cause and Effect is the building block of the universe. Every effect has a cause, just as every cause has an effect. And the original, primary level of cause is thought. In other words, thought is the initial cause of everything that happens, and thought is the initial cause of any effort to change it. We read in the book of Genesis that the world began when "God spoke." His thoughts created the universe, and continually recreate it.

Thoughts of love are cause with a capital *C;* thoughts of fear are cause with a little *c.* *C* thoughts have dominion over *c* thoughts, because love is real and fear is not; love comes from God, fear does not. Any appearance produced by fear-based thinking is happening only within the worldly illusion, and illusions cannot stand in the presence of love.

We experience who we really are, and what it is we're meant to do, in any moment when we pour our love into the universe.

Your natural state is external prosperity, because your internal state is spiritually prosperous. By external prosperity I don't necessarily mean great wealth as the world defines it, but a level of material sustenance that does not include lack or fear.

Beyond the veil of illusion that is our perceptual framework lies a universe of miracles. That universe is not a dream world. It is our spiritual home to which we are destined to return—not at some later date, after we die or after many lifetimes of effort, but *every instant of our lives.* Our heart is the compass that leads us there. The universe of miracles is where our soul truly lives, even in our mortal forgetfulness. It is not a metaphor, but an actual dimension of consciousness. It is the holy grail of the spiritual quest.

A shift in thinking from fear to love *is* the miracle. A miracle is not a supernatural event. It is metaphysical. ("Meta" means *beyond:* thus metaphysical reality refers to a reality that is beyond the physical.) There is nothing supernatural about love or its effects; in fact, love is our true natural state of being. The thinking of the world is simply upside down, with the naturalness of love feeling almost unnatural at times and the unnaturalness of fear feeling natural. The most powerful, liberating thing we can do is to break from the fear-based thinking that dominates the world—to surrender the mind-set the world has taught us and accept a new one instead.

• • •

THERE ARE TIMES when what we thought was our very best thinking drove us straight into a ditch. Sometimes, though we played what we thought were our best cards, we still went bust. We did what we thought we should do, and we still lost everything. We tried our best, and we still ended up with disaster looming.

That's when we're ready to do the one thing we've been terrified to do: admit to ourselves that we're out of ideas, that we need help we're incapable of providing for ourselves. Then we find—somewhere around the time when our knees hit the floor—that this isn't when it's all *over;* this is when it all *begins.* What begins? Our awareness of who we really are, Who walks with us, and why we're here.

We experience who we really are, and what it is we're meant to do, in any moment when we pour our love into the universe. That's the moment when we finally "arrive," cultivating an attitude in which we see ourselves as here to serve a greater plan than our own, as vessels through which the love that is the heart of all things flows through us to bless the world. This isn't something to announce to everyone we meet, obviously, but it's something that any of us can think about and act on.

Opening ourselves fully to love is much different than the "success mentality" taught by the world. No taking the bull by the horns, no trying to push other people out of the way so you can be number one, no desperate struggling to get to the top of the heap. As children of God, each of us already *is* at the top of the heap. The only real top of the heap is love, and love is what we are.

In recognizing that you're here only to love, you realize that as long as you do that, you're already a success. And love doesn't have to be something grand. As Mother Teresa said, "There are no great deeds; there are just small deeds done with great love." It might be a kinder greeting to the checkout person at the grocery store, or an apology to someone whose feelings you've hurt, or a simple expression of kindness, compassion, or forgiveness.

The point isn't just what you give when you love, but also what you open yourself to receive. As you send love out, the universe will send love back. It's simply the Law of Cause and Effect.

• • •

WHEN WE THINK of ourselves as channels for the infinite creative energy of the universe, we think higher thoughts than "How will I get a job?" We're lifted to a realm of consciousness where questions like "How can I best serve the world?" take precedence over "What can I get out of this?" Within that realm, we naturally *do* get a job, we naturally *do* create money, and we naturally *do* produce an outer prosperity that reflects the prosperity in our hearts. This doesn't mean we don't have to do the footwork. But our feet become guided by a wisdom we might not have even known we had.

We do this not just to make money or even to get employment; we do this in order to live in the flow of a meaningful, joyful life. In a very real way, money is the least of it. We're here to do work that exists on a higher plane than mere money. That doesn't mean money isn't to be respected, or dealt with appropriately, responsibly, and with moderation. It is, and we will suffer accordingly when we fail to remember that. But money itself is neither good nor bad. It is a material thing that, like all material things, is infused with holiness *if created righteously and used for holy purposes.*

The way to abundance is to surrender our abilities and talents, asking that they be used by God to help heal the world. Too many people feel that they have talent but simply don't know where to put it. We're not raised in a society that asks, "What are your gifts, and how can they make the world a more beautiful place?" We're usually asked something more like this: "What will you do to make a living?" This knocks us out of our natural rhythm, because the soul simply doesn't think that way. There is no more natural proclivity than to serve love. Something very powerful happens when we pray, "Dear God, please use me." Making ourselves available to the universe for its loving purposes, we are taken up on our offer immediately.

When anything—money included—is separated from our natural proclivities, the miraculous universe is thrown off course. As long as we make love our bottom line, then our lives will naturally prosper. Sometimes, what will later make us a fortune arrives first as a creative impulse that no one would necessarily think profitable at the time. Do something not because you think it might make money; do it because it makes your heart sing. The biblical injunction "Seek ye first the kingdom of heaven and all else will be added unto you" means "Embrace the realization of your oneness with all things, and everything that could contribute to your good will emerge from the power of that thought."

One day, you might find yourself called to a task that makes no money at all. But if it contributes to your stature as a human being, to your character and integrity; if it teaches you about yourself and the world; if it provides you an opportunity to show up fully for life—then it was a prosperous activity. Another day, you might find yourself in a job you don't really love, and yet if you're honest with yourself you realize it's teaching you discipline, or humility, or responsibility— necessary lessons in order to attract and manage money correctly.

Money comes from the universe and will arrive when it's created, not just by a material cause but by the energy of righteousness. Righteousness means "right use" of the mind, and the only right use of the mind is love.

The universe knows what our needs are and is programmed to provide for them. When you start asking, "Have I provided for love's needs?" more frequently than you ask, "Has love provided for *my* needs?" then the miracles that occur naturally in the presence of love will fall at your feet and into your hands.

To the ego mind, surrender means giving up. To the spiritual mind, surrender means giving in and receiving. Once we're there, inside the holy place where all is inner riches, the outer gold of worldly prosperity appears in a miraculous way. It comes inviting us to use our wealth responsibly and to share it generously, as the universe so shared it with us.

Dear God,

I surrender to You who I am, what I have and what I do.

May my life and talents be used in whatever way serves You best.

I surrender to You my failures and any pain still in my heart.

I surrender to You my successes, and the hopes that they contain.

May the Light of Your Love shine deep within my heart,

and extend through me to bless the world.

Amen.

CHAPTER 9

Transcending Fear

None of this "love and it will all be okay" stuff sounds attractive, or even sane, to the ego mind.

Yet our spiritual task in life is to overcome the ego. The ego is the mind of fear. It is our own mental power turned against ourselves. It is the part of us that thinks that we have to struggle to get ahead, that we must compete with everyone else, that there is only so much success to go around.

But the ego mind is not the truth of who we are, and what it says is not true. It is our own self-hatred masquerading as self-love. The ego purports to help us while actually luring us into the anxious hell of confused and confusing thoughts.

The ego consists of—and perpetuates—the chronic, self-destructive patterns by which we sabotage ourselves, blow opportunities, destroy relationships, and undermine ourselves in a myriad of ways. Yet these self-defeating patterns don't announce themselves as such. The ego is very seductive. It comes in the guise of responsible considerations, telling us something is reasonable that only later we realize wasn't reasonable at all; it just seemed, for some insane reason, like a good idea at the time.

The ego, or fear-mind, is the false belief that we are separate from God.

The egoic fear-based thinking of the world (which is 180 degrees away from the thinking of God) falls like a veil in front of our eyes, obscuring what is real. So how do we transcend the ego and lift the veil? This veil of illusion is automatically lifted when we remember who we are and why we're here. The key to power in any situation is to be clear about two things: Who am I, really? And why am I here? Those two questions, answered correctly, give you the power to work miracles.

Your mind is holy, because it is a creation of God. It was created for the purpose of extending His love into the world. Your work is geared to success to the extent that it is dedicated to love's purposes. Remember this, and your mind will be filled with an impenetrable power.

Until and unless we align ourselves with spiritual truth, we are vulnerable to ego thoughts. According to *A Course in Miracles,* with every thought we are either host to God or hostage to the ego.

I remember years ago telling myself I didn't have to worry about the devil. I had realized that there was no evil force out there stalking the planet for human souls, that that idea was all in my mind. But then I realized that this is *the worst place it could possibly be.* It's not like good news or something that the only place darkness exists is inside your head.

The ego is a constant temptation, dwelling in all of us, to perceive without love. It creates a limita-

tion; then it would have us believe that the limitation is insurmountable. It manufactures a problem;
then it would convince us that the problem is intractable. The fact that the ego is inside your mind
in no way means that it's your friend. On the other
hand, the fact that it's inside your mind means that
you yourself can change it!

A MAN AT one of my lectures once told me that
he'd lived a happy life as a piano teacher, but with
the recession hitting people so hard, he wasn't
teaching enough students to be able to make a
living. Dan said he had prayed for a miracle.

So far, so good. Not long afterward, he received notification about a job that had opened
up in an educational institution near where he
lived, a job that seemed to fit his qualifications.
He had been highly recommended for the position and felt certain that he had a good chance
of getting it.

Okay. Still so far, so good. The Law of Divine
Compensation seemed to be doing its thing. But
then the ego went to work.

Here is how Dan described his process of thinking: The problem, he told himself, was that such jobs as this are too political, too fraught with institutional drama, and he would have to play a certain kind of game in order to vie for the position. After much consideration, he decided not to apply.

Notice how the ego wormed its way into his thinking: *Yes, I prayed for a miracle, but I decided that what came my way wasn't good enough. If it were really a miracle, it would look exactly as I had imagined it.* Judgment set in, and the miracle was blocked.

Notice how sly the ego is here, deflecting the opportunity in the name of *values*. It would have him think that his fear-based choice was somehow ethically superior.

What would a miracle-minded process look like instead? First, once you pray for a miracle, consider it done. Second, be alert for the universe to show you an opportunity, *even if it doesn't look like what you'd expect.* The fact that a possible solution to your problem comes in a form that your ego hadn't planned is usually more rather than less of a sign that it's coming from God.

I asked Dan how he could be sure politics would actually be involved. The scuttlebutt on the street that the situation was "political" was based on past situations that didn't even pertain to him. It wasn't necessarily true, and even if it had been, it didn't have to apply to him in the present.

How could he be certain of what this situation might be before he even opened himself to the experience? He was like someone whose doorbell rang and who, without even opening the door, presumed to know who was on the other side, what that person was wearing, and what he or she was there for—so he decided not to open the door!

It's not enough that miracles are always coming at us; we must be receptive, or "miracle-ready." To receive miracles, we must have an open mind as well as an open heart. The ego would close both.

Being open to miracles is a discipline and an art. We should beware of thinking that we'll know what a miracle will look like, what shape it will take, or what form it will come in; in fact, the very nature of miracles is that they represent the interruption of a pattern, a discontinuation of the status quo. The Law of Divine Compensation forges a new trajectory, one that isn't based on the past but rather only on God's love for you. God does not know of limits, nor bow before the ego's dictates of scarcity and lack. He doesn't share the ego's shabby assessment of you, and neither should you.

How do we get rid of our mental intruder? The ego isn't something *to* get rid of, because in actuality it doesn't exist. It's simply a mortal hallucination that we've all bought into. It is the absence of love, the same way darkness is the absence of light. When we turn on light, darkness disappears; and when we turn on love, the ego disappears. Whatever we devote to truth will be able to withstand lies.

ACCORDING TO *A Course in Miracles,* we think we have many different problems, but we really have only one: our separation from God.

Several years ago, after one of my talks, a man came up to me and said, "All this 'lean on God' stuff isn't me." I told him that, in my own life, whenever I *haven't* leaned on God, I've found myself leaning on something or someone I'd have been better off not leaning on!

It is not a weakness to lean on the power of the universe that resides within us. It is a myth that we can be the lone hero, not depending on anyone or anything else. The soul *leans*. That is part of its nature.

Idolatry is when we lean on something or someone that is not in fact the source of our ultimate good, thinking for some insane reason that it is. This is an almost inevitable temptation for all of us, living as we do in a world where the material plane is deemed the only true reality.

This mistaken thought—that the material world is our salvation—is the insanity at the heart of all error. It is the ego's central delusion. In our work lives, this delusion can lead to various errors: fear masquerades as humility; irresponsible behavior masquerades as reasonable risk; overspending masquerades as an attitude of abundance; unethical advertising masquerades as "no big deal;" financial shenanigans masquerade as merely "how things are done."

Our connection to the spiritual plane is the antidote to the ego's insanity. It gives us a sense of wisdom, scale, and righteousness. It gives us confidence and power. It is the prayer that our work be used by God to make the world a better place.

Bob Dylan captured this truth in his song "Gotta Serve Somebody": "It may be the devil or it may be the Lord / but you're gonna have to serve somebody." Not serving someone or something is not an option. Pray to serve the universe, and the universe will serve you.

That which is proactively placed in the service of love is protected from the grips of fear. That which is proactively placed in the service of deep sanity is protected from the grips of neurosis. That which is proactively placed in the service of what is good, holy, and beautiful is protected from the forces of destruction.

Take yourself, your work, and the God within you seriously—dedicate yourself daily, hourly, even moment by moment to love's purposes—and the ego won't have a chance. It knows a holy mind when it sees one.

Dear God,
I dedicate to You my talents and abilities.
May they be used in a way that serves Your
purposes.
I surrender to You my business and finances.
May my work be lifted to its highest possibility,
As a blessing on all the world.
Amen.

CHAPTER 10

Positivity

Most people realize the deleterious effects of negativity in the workplace; whining, complaining, anger, and general nay-saying create obvious barriers to accomplishment. Whether it's an individual complaining that the system "won't let me succeed," or someone piping up to insist that a creative idea "simply can't be done, so let's not even talk about it," negative attitudes stop miracles in their tracks.

While the power of negativity is clear to most everyone, the power of vigorous positivity receives short shrift in comparison. Positivity is more than the absence of the negative; it is the presence—through thought, word, and action—of the positive. In other words, simply not being negative is not enough. If we're interested in creating miracles, in invoking the most powerful creative manifestation, we must proactively *be positive*. There are three types of positive attitude that make all the difference: positivity about other people, positivity about possibility, and positivity about ourselves.

LET'S BEGIN BY looking at positivity about other people. After all, few of us achieve anything by ourselves. An array of employers, employees, colleagues, associates, customers, and so forth form a matrix of relationships at the heart of any worldly success.

Think of your work life, therefore, not as *separate* from your spiritual life but as *central* to your spiritual life. Whatever your business, it is your ministry.

Every relationship either gives energy to us or withholds energy from us, according to what we give to or withhold from it. And it's not only our behavior toward others, but our very thoughts about them, that builds and/or destroys relationships. Since all minds are joined, everyone subconsciously knows everything. Thinking positively about those we work with (or would like to work with) has a miraculous power. When we think of someone with love, we are making soul contact, thus invoking the expression of that person's highest self. That in turn increases the possibility that he or she will meet us on the level of our own highest self, bringing greater chances of high-level synergy and creativity between us.

Thinking lovingly about someone is a far more sophisticated measure than simply visualizing a positive outcome of a business relationship. In fact, that's not even so positive, necessarily, unless our core intention is service to the other. Thinking positively about someone spiritually means blessing that person, praying for his or her happiness, and praying that we be an instrument of greater good in that person's life.

No matter what situation brings people together, on the spiritual plane every relationship is an assignment. We're brought together by an intentional universe for one reason only: the enlightenment of all concerned. Whether our connection is through work or family, a casual encounter or a lifelong involvement, the purpose of every relationship is the healing of the world.

The ego would separate our thoughts of work from our thoughts of the sacred, positing that work is material and God is spiritual, and therefore the twain do not meet. Since the world itself is merely a projection of our thoughts, however, there is no ultimate separation between our *spirit,* i.e., loving thought, and anything that we *do.* Separating our thoughts of work from our thoughts of spiritual devotion is thus personally disempowering, because it throws us out of the spirit mind and into fear. In fear, we forget who we really are. Forgetting who we are, we forget Who lives within us. And in forgetting Who lives within us, we lose conscious connection to our power. Through remembering Who lives within us, and dedicating ourselves to His purposes, we achieve miraculous results.

Think of your work life, therefore, not as *separate* from your spiritual life but as *central* to your spiritual life. Whatever your business, it is your ministry. Every relationship, every activity, every circumstance is part of your ministry, to the extent that you think of it that way. Such devotion uplifts the vibration of your thinking, thus improving the experience that others have of you and that you have of them.

Through our physical eyes, a group of people working together are seen as discrete and separate entities, related only through the sheer coincidence that they happen to all be working at the same place at the same time. Indeed, if this were a random universe, then that would be so.

But it is *not* a random universe, and everyone is wherever he or she is through divine assignment. That assignment does not necessarily mean that the situation should remain as it is: sometimes love's lesson is learning to say no. But one way or another, there is meaning to everything that occurs. Lessons come in many different forms, and for everyone in a situation, the lesson is different. For one person, the lesson might be to contribute more. For another, the lesson might be to be kinder. For one, it might be to listen more. For another, it might be to speak up more. For another, it may even be to leave. No matter what the circumstance, however, working together is an opportunity for growth for everyone involved. And all growth is a conduit of miracles.

I once attended a business meeting with a group of people trying to get a new project off the ground. The conversation centered on money: Where were they going to get money? How would they raise money to fund the project? How could they get people to invest?

Sitting with the group, I kept thinking how much hidden gold was right there at the conference table. The gold was simply not mined—in fact, no one seemed to realize it was even there. Every person at the table carried within them priceless treasures in the form of ideas and creativity. How do I know this? Because as children of God, *we all do.*

Modern civilization hasn't scratched the surface of truly liberating our human potential, because an overly secular worldview doesn't *recognize* the deepest human potential. As a consequence, we continue to project onto external sources—money and what it can buy—the idolatrous notion that we need those sources in order to create success. In fact, it's the other way around. It's when we open the doors to true success—sharing our passion and ideas in service to a higher good, each person invited to express his or her unique contribution to the whole—that any material means necessary to support the work will be miraculously brought forward by a self-organizing universe. Once the energy is potent enough, the business deal will arrive by itself.

Energy can create wealth, but wealth of itself cannot create energy. No amount of money, technology, or strategy can equal the value of passionate people brainstorming new possibilities. Material wealth emerges from the nonmaterial source of human imagination and passion—passion for an idea, a purpose, a possibility of something as yet unseen. Such passion cannot be bought, but only inspired. A salary alone does not generate human enthusiasm, at least not for long. Human enthusiasm isn't *created by* money so much as it *creates* money.

Yet there was no container at that conference table into which people could pour their hearts, much less their ideas. No one was asking them about themselves, or their deeper creative visions. What was missing, ironically, was something that costs no money at all: the consciousness of genuine concern. That concern is the essence of true leadership. A real leader is not the top dog who merely shouts down orders. A leader is one who holds the space for the brilliance of others.

Many years ago, a young man who worked for me spoke about his job this way: "We're over there across the street, making the audiotapes, and no one ever comes over to ask us how we are or even notice that we exist." I was stunned. An elephant had been sitting next to me that I hadn't even realized was in the room.

What had I been thinking, exactly? If someone on my team could be that unhappy, that untended to, how could I think that this enterprise was really going to *produce* in the world? In the words of Mahatma Gandhi, "the end is inherent in the means." No company or organization filled with unhappy people will ultimately rise to its highest potential.

We're all selective with our application of spiritual principles until we're not, and for years I failed to see the ministry aspect of the workplace itself. I had a profound concern for my audience and their needs, yet a twisted view of what I owed or didn't owe to people who were there to help me serve them.

Our workplace can be the ego's lair, or the spirit's sanctuary. It can be an easy home for attitudes of disrespect, entitlement, arrogance, laziness, exploitation, disloyalty, and greed. But the workplace can also be a beautiful home for the most positive energies, should we proactively choose to express them. Our egos are more vigilant in monitoring the sins of others than in identifying our own; we're quick to point out where we think others are making mistakes and sometimes slow to look at our own. The employer finds it easier to blame the employee; the employee finds it easier to blame the employer. The seeker, on the other hand, seeks no blame at all, but simply understanding and transformation.

As for the young man who told me I didn't seem to care whether or not he existed, his comment opened up a floodgate of realization on my part.

I had failed him as an employer, and I knew it. It took me years to understand that every workplace should be a *positivity team*. Every employee has a right to feel appreciated for his or her gifts, and every employer has a right to expect the highest standards of excellence.

How might the leader of the business meeting mentioned above have mined the gold of his employees? Before he went into the meeting, he might have said a prayer for everyone who was going to be at the meeting, or saluted them internally in whatever way was true for him. During the meeting, he could have looked at everyone in turn, thinking, "The love in me salutes the love in you." (Obviously, it wouldn't have been appropriate to say such a thing aloud!) No one would have known, on a conscious level, that anything at all had occurred. But on an invisible, miraculous level, everyone at the table would have been lifted into a higher psychological and emotional alignment. Having been inwardly saluted, the group members would have felt invited to share their gifts.

If you're interested in building a positivity team, let's start now:

Write down on a piece of paper every person with whom you've worked in your past—employees, employers, coworkers, customers, agents, clients, and so forth. Closing your eyes, allow them to appear in your imagination like a queue of people waiting in line at a movie. For that's exactly what they were, except that they weren't lining up to *see* a movie; they were lining up to *be in* a movie: the movie of *your life*!

As you think of those individuals from your past, remember that every relationship is an assignment, in which people are drawn together because they represent a maximal and mutual opportunity for soul growth. Whether you liked particular individuals or not is irrelevant; whether they liked you or not is irrelevant. What is relevant is that you see now whatever lesson you might have failed to learn before, so that you will have no need to repeat it.

Within the inner space of your mind, bow before every person standing in the line. Within your heart, bless, apologize, and forgive wherever necessary. And complete forgiveness *is* necessary, if we're to attract and produce miracles. Thank each person for the blessing he or she gave you, even if the blessing was in the form of a lesson learned.

With each one, ask yourself, Did I do my best? Could I have done better? Could I have acted differently? And then place each relationship into the hands of God.

Now see another line of people, some of whom were also in the first line: everyone you're working with or could be working with now. Inwardly, bow before the spirit of each one. Acknowledge their gifts and thank them for what they have done for you. Fill your heart with an attitude of appreciation. Pray to be a vessel of love that invokes their fulfillment and joy.

Now imagine the people you would *like* to work with: people you would love to collaborate with or work for. Know that they may or may not be the actual ones who are meant to be on your path in life; they may simply represent an image of the kinds of people who are doing the kinds of projects you yearn to be part of. Whatever the vision, honor it and surrender it to God. Pray that your energy expand to such an extent that it would be *natural* for you to find yourself in a room with such people, working and creating with them. The only barriers that exist are the barriers within your mind. Seek to remove your barriers to love, and miracles will replace them. The barriers will disappear into the nothingness from whence they came.

Perhaps you can pray with your work team, but perhaps it wouldn't be appropriate. Either way, *you* can pray each day for the happiness and fulfillment of everyone you work with or wish to work with. Having done that, you will have done your part. Miracles will follow.

THE SECOND TYPE of positivity concerns how we view possibility. A man named Jonathon came to me one day quite depressed about money problems. He always seemed to just scrape by, he said, and he wasn't even doing with his life what he really wanted to do. He worked as a carpenter, yet he longed to be a musician. He was always putting out financial fires—in fact, he was now facing a tax bill larger than he could pay—and he never seemed to get it together as a musician.

He said to me numerous times as we spoke, "I have an issue about being taken care of. I never think that there will be enough." My eyes usually glaze over when I hear such explanations—first, because they're self-fulfilling prophecies, and second, because the miracle is never in the past but in the present. In God's universe there is always enough.

The more I inquired about Jonathon's circumstances, the more I discovered that he was not just a carpenter, he was considered an excellent carpenter; yet he turned down most jobs he was offered. He did this, he told me, because he really wanted to be a musician and he didn't want to give the universe the wrong message. He figured that if he did too much carpentry work, his possibilities of a musical career would dry up.

I pointed out that from what he was telling me, there *were* no musical opportunities at the moment, yet there *was* a tax bill! Metaphysically, it didn't make sense to argue that if he worked to make money to pay his bills, the universe would reward him by closing doors. Quite the opposite: any time we show up for life with integrity and impeccability, doors open.

The part of the story that most caught my attention was the fact that while he had been praying for money, he had been turning down work! It's like the old story of the man who found himself in a storm, with floodwater rising around him, and prayed to be rescued, yet turned down offered rides in a car, a boat, and finally even a helicopter, claiming, "God will take care of me." Soon he drowned and went to heaven. Upon meeting God he upbraided Him, complaining that in his hour of need God had not been there for him. To which God responded, "What do you mean, I wasn't there for you?! I sent a car; I sent a boat; I sent a helicopter . . . !"

Jonathon, it seemed to me, had an odd concept of "being taken care of." We *are* taken care of, but as the saying goes, "God helps those who help themselves." It's a cliché because it's so often said, but it's so often said because it's true.

Native Americans recognized that wherever there was a poison in the forest, an antidote to the poison could be found within several feet. Usually, what we're looking for is on some level right in front of us. The universe is wired to give us what we need, yet we have to show up for the experience of life with a positive attitude in order to experience its gifts. I've known people who seemed to think that waking up in the morning, driving to work, and showing up at their desk should be enough. Well, it's not. Our attitude—a willingness to bring all our emotional, psychological, material, and intellectual resources to a job—makes all the difference. It's not just what a job brings to us that matters, but what we bring to a job. "I'll do whatever it takes"—and yes, even sometimes "I'm willing to do windows"—is the attitude of a winner, not a loser.

Jonathon saw carpentry as somehow beneath him, not recognizing what seemed to me to be an obvious gift that had been laid in front of him. His succeeding as a carpenter wouldn't limit his possibilities as a musician; carpentry was a way to make money, pay off his bills, and have some cash so he could support himself while he pursued whatever dreams were in his heart. By disparaging his own work, he was limiting the possibilities in front of him. That shift in perception would be his miracle.

It doesn't matter whether we're contributing to the universe as a carpenter or a musician, a teacher or an artist, a janitor or a caretaker, a parent or a

POSITIVITY

salesperson. What matters is our consciousness while we're doing it: our willingness to be of service in whatever way is presented, seeing nothing as either above us or beneath us, yet important because it's in front of us.

We should never say yes or no to anything without reflection and contemplation. For the higher purpose of a situation is not always obvious, but it is always there. In a universe where God's handwriting is everywhere, we never have to worry that life will lead us away from our greater good. It will always lead us into our greater good, as we proactively and positively bring to it the fullness of ourselves.

THE THIRD TYPE of positivity concerns how we look at ourselves. *A Course in Miracles* tells us that all the children of God are special, and none of the children of God are special. We're all imbued with the same potential brilliance, because we're all imbued with the spirit of God. Thinking that *your* talent or *your* abilities make *you* special will produce fear, because such thinking posits a separation between you and others. Separation between you and others means separation between you and God, and separation from God produces not power, but rather a hidden hysteria. "I'm better than anyone else" is not actually a success-oriented thought form; "I'm personally no big deal, but I'm here so I guess I'm the one who's supposed to be channeling the genius of God in this particular situation" is better. It's humble, not arrogant, to realize that the genius of God lies within you. Just remember that the genius itself is not in you any more than in anyone else.

Our job isn't to create our genius—we *couldn't,* by the way—but to make ourselves available to God's. Yes, we must work at what we do, make efforts to improve our skills and so forth, for spirit can channel only through a prepared vessel. But once we've made the preparations we're called to make, we can surrender the ultimate performance of a task and allow the Holy Spirit to flow through us.

Our power as miracle-workers in the workplace is to pray that we be used—that our hands, our feet, our minds, and our behavior be of service to a greater good. That we be empty vessels through which God will produce His extraordinary wonders. We're simply here to serve a higher plan for the enlightenment of the world, and therein lie our happiness and success.

A friend of mine is a brilliant television writer. I've read her scripts and I'm blown away each time. But when she talks about having to pitch one of those scripts to a TV network executive, you'd think she was about to get twenty cavities filled with no Novocain. It's one thing to work like the consummate professional she is, on the writing itself; that, I admire greatly. But the angst and nervousness before every pitch meeting; that, I question. For the One who sourced the writing will also lead the meeting, if she will let Him! In *A Course in Miracles,* it's written that we should be less concerned about our own readiness, and more consistently aware of His.

There is a story in the Gospel of Thomas in which Jesus tells his disciples to go into the countryside and "teach the gospel" (by which he meant simply, "demonstrate love"). Wanting more specific direction, they ask him what they should say, to which he responds, "I'll tell you when you get there."

Think about that story in light of my script-writer friend. Her most powerful preparation for a meeting with a TV executive would be, obviously, to write the best script possible. But after that? Surrender the meeting. Pray for whoever is going to be there. Ask that everything that happens in the meeting serve the highest creative possibility for all concerned. Know that she doesn't have to decide in advance every word she's going to say at the meeting, because He Who lives within her will reveal all things with a miraculous quality she can't possibly formulate with her rational mind.

Her greatest power lay in emptying her mind of all thoughts—aiming for the Zen "beginner's mind"—and praying that they be replaced by His. Once she'd done her work and had all the information she needed in her conscious mind, her subconscious could take it from there. Her mind could formulate a pitch, but only her spirit could be inspired and inspire others.

In summation, there are four rules for miraculous work creation: Be positive. Send love. Have fun. Kick ass.

Amen.

CHAPTER 11

Job vs. Calling

One of the most positive transitions you can make is from viewing your work as a job to viewing it as a calling. A job is an exchange of energy in which you do a material task and someone provides money in exchange. A calling, however, is an organic field of energy that emerges from the deepest aspects of who you are. It is the fulfillment of what God has created you to be and do. Approaching your work as a job versus approaching it as a calling makes all the difference in whether or not you dwell in the miraculous universe.

You have a calling simply because you are alive. You have a calling because you are a child of God. You have a calling because you're on this earth with a divine purpose: to rise to the level of your highest creative possibility, expressing all that you are intellectually, emotionally, psychologically, and physically in order to make the universe a more beautiful place.

As you do this, your entire life becomes your ministry—a way to serve God and to serve the world.

The best way to summon your true calling is to put yourself in service to God.

If you're thinking of money only as something you get in exchange for doing a job, then you'll never be free of limited thought forms surrounding money. We are heir to the laws that rule the world we identify with. If you identify only with the material plane, you place yourself at the effect of pretty severe economic realities of scarcity and lack. If you identify with the spiritual plane, you're under no laws but God's.

"I'm looking for a job," "I'm trying to figure out what I should do," and "I don't know how I'm going to make ends meet" are sentences that confuse the universe. A child of God doesn't have to "look for a job"; a child of God doesn't have to "figure out what to do"; a child of God doesn't have to worry about "how to make ends meet." A child of God is simply a magnet for all things good. The *you* who thinks of life as a struggle, or a place where you're on your own, is not the real you. The real you already has a God-given function, and the universe is set up to support it.

The best way to summon your true calling is to put yourself in service to God. The following daily prayer is from *A Course in Miracles:* "Where would you have me go? What would you have me do? What would you have me say, and to whom?"

While a job is separate from the rest of our lives, a calling is a *fulfillment* of the rest of our lives. By striving to *be* the best we can be, we create the internal blueprint by which we *do* the best we can do. On a soul level, we *want* to work, we *want* to create, we *want* to be productive and serve others and share our gifts with the world.

Often it is not external forms of obstruction that hold us back, but rather internal ones. And nothing releases us internally more than the desire and the willingness to serve.

The world can give you a job, and a job can be taken away. But a true calling puts you in a career zone that cannot be taken away. It reflects your willingness to do what you feel inwardly led to do in order to help heal the world. The universe then registers your true substance, your true seriousness, and your true purpose.

Some things you do will bring forth worldly wealth; other things you do will not directly bring forth wealth at all, but—being the right things to do—will summon wealth miraculously from other sources.

Losing a job does not mean losing your calling, because as a personal ambassador of God, you have been given a permanent assignment. You are here to represent Him who sent you, and He does not change His mind about you. You are never unemployed by God. And that's true not just about you; it's true about all of us.

Anything that appears to separate us from each other is not the deepest level of our identity. We all have different jobs, but the same ministry. Some of us are technicians, some of us are mathematicians, some of us are writers and artists, some of us are salespeople, some of us don't even work as work is defined by the world—but our value, individually, is determined not by what we do but by the consciousness with which we do it.

We're all here to be available channels for the love that heals all things. A job takes a *form,* but our ministry is *content.* Even if you lose your job, you still have your ministry, because it is part of who you are. Your life has no less value if you're not employed as the world defines it. If you're kind to people, if you're compassionate, if you pour your excellence into whatever you're doing, then you're doing the job God sent you to do. From that will emerge the next form that's needed to host the energies you're bringing forth.

Does that mean you don't have to "look for a job" as the world defines it? Of course you do! But you do it with a different consciousness. You don't show up for a job interview thinking, "How do I impress them? I really need this job." Rather, your process goes more like this:

1. You place your need for work in God's hands.

Surrendering a situation to God means surrendering your *thoughts* about it. You're programming your mind to think thoughts that are the most creative, positive, insightful, and beneficial. You're not giving up responsibility or turning your power over to something outside yourself; you're taking the *highest* responsibility for your circumstances, asking God to make your mind a literal touchstone for miraculous breakthroughs. You walk forward in confidence that God provides.

2. While alert to every opportunity that presents itself, you put enthusiastic energy into brainstorming and creating new possibilities.

You remember that the universe is infinitely abundant, like an orchard filled with fruit that's just for you. But if you're hungry, you can't simply look at an orchard from the side of the road! The universe brought you the orchard; you yourself have to pick the fruit. You are willing to meet opportunity with positivity and faith.

3. You pray and meditate, asking for internal guidance as to whom to call, what to do, and so forth.

When you meditate and pray, you literally emit different brain waves. You receive impulses of insight and creativity that do not flow easily into an anxious mind. You enter the internal temple, the engine room from which you generate the probabilities of success. "I'm too anxious to meditate" is one of the most self-sabotaging things we can say. When we meditate, we stop *being* anxious.

4. You realize that you can't know what or where your next job should be.

You trust that there is a perfect plan for the unfolding of your highest good, which your rational mind cannot formulate. God's plan works, and yours doesn't. You cannot know how your part fits best into a larger plan for the healing of the world, but God does. Your job is merely to open your mind and open your heart so that a higher consciousness can then flow through you.

5. Before you go to a job interview, audition, or meeting, you blast every person you're going to be with—and the situation itself—with light and love.

Your goal becomes simply giving and receiving love—which is another way of saying, "May God's will be done." You see every interaction as a holy encounter. You intend for this and every situation to be one in which you express your truest, most brilliant, most loving self—and what happens beyond that, you leave to the intelligence of the universe. You're not going to the interview to try to *get* a job; you're going there to *do* your job!

Those five steps might seem as if they are just little things—hardly the operating principles that move the universe. Yet that is exactly what they are.

· · ·

ON THE SPIRITUAL plane, you have no competitors. There is no competition for your position, as you are a unique expression of the Mind of God. You not only have a place in the universe; you have an essential *function* in the universe. Only you can do the job of being you, and the universe itself is left incomplete without you. It is not arrogant but humble to realize this, as you place yourself in service to the greatest drama there is: the actualization of your own potential.

Your highest function is simply to be the person you are capable of being, and from that effort—the development of your kindness and positivity, your vulnerability and availability to life—your calling will emerge.

As you become who you are meant to be, what you are meant to do will fall like a path of rose petals before you. You may be thinking, "I don't *know* what my calling is," but God does. He knows how your talents and abilities can best fit into His plan for the enlightenment and healing of all things. What talents you have, He will glorify as you use them to glorify Him. And talents you don't even know that you have, that lie latent within you, will emerge as you surrender more deeply to love.

Your calling is what you would do whether you were paid to do it or not. Your calling is what you *have* to do in order to be happy. Your calling is what connects you to your deepest self, and to the rest of life around you. If you have no idea what that would be, simply pray, "Dear God, please use me," and awareness of your calling will appear miraculously.

From the time she was a little girl, my daughter was entranced by stories of historical kings and queens. Constantly she would say to me, "Mommy, tell me a queen story." Even when very young, she would read books about King Henry VIII and his wives, following me around the house telling me about this or that historical incident. Now she's a graduate student in history. While some have suggested to me that finding a job as a history professor might not be easy once she graduates, I never worry that she won't be able to make a living as a historian, because history isn't just a job to her. History is her calling. She is genuinely *excited* about it. Whether she pursues her love of history as a professor or writer, or shares her knowledge via some other means, her passion will undoubtedly make her of use to the world. I have no doubt that in the miraculous universe, she will be compensated appropriately for the work she does.

I'm always sad to hear parents saying to their child, "But how will you make a living doing *that*?" when their child is obviously passionate about something. Reading the biography of Steve Jobs, anyone can see that this kid with a love of computers, working away in his parents' garage, wasn't thinking just about how he would get a job. He was responding to a higher calling—a calling for the ages, as it turned out—and no one doubts the abundance that he created. Not all of us have the talent of a computer genius, but all of us have a call to greatness nonetheless.

The true you, your holy self, is beyond any limits of the mortal world. So are the talents and brilliance within you. When you dwell in that knowledge, simply recognizing and appreciating the divine spirit residing in all of us, you receive the charisma of a self-confident person.

Someone who has confidence in God comes across as confident to the world; someone who thinks of him- or herself as a follower of God comes across as a leader to the world. You'll develop a kind of invisible light, a sense of humble certitude, a greatness that comes from beyond yourself. Your abilities, your intelligence, your talents, your personality, your circumstances, your dreams will all come together in a beautiful pattern. And you will see all this as your calling—a calling back and forth, in continuous song, from your heart to the universe and the universe back to you.

In the words of Confucius, "Choose a job you love, and you will never have to work a day in your life."

CHAPTER 12

Embracing Abundance

As a child of God, you are inwardly abundant. External abundance is simply a reflection of who and what you are.

A spiritual economy is one in which abundance is a natural result of people actualizing their God-given gifts. True prosperity is the prospering of our spirits in service to love.

You are an idea in the Mind of God, and an idea does not leave its source. God is infinite and God is love; therefore you share in that infinitude and you share in that love. This is simply the truth of who you are.

The universe of which you are part is an all-loving field of miraculous possibility, not only in every instant but also moving through time. In physics terms, you're not a particle but a wave. You're not a static thing, but rather an ever-evolving emanation of the Mind of God. Spirit has great plans for you, because God's Mind is an eternal wellspring of infinite love. This wellspring literally never runs out of ideas.

We feel it would be arrogant to think of ourselves as "God's gift to the world," yet in fact that's exactly who each of us is.

Your awareness of these things helps right the universe on your behalf, lifting you above the effects of the fear-based thought system that dominates this planet. Your greatest source of power in this world is the knowledge that you're not *of* this world. None of us are truly at home in this dimension, and—counterintuitive though it is—we dwell most comfortably within the world when we know that. Our true home lies beyond the veil of illusion, and we are here to shed the light of our true home into all darkened corners of the world. With that understanding we unleash the unlimited potential that lies within each of us to create the good, the true, and the beautiful.

Such are the gifts of the spirit that we carry within. We're programmed *for* abundance because we *are* abundant. Financial prosperity is one of the many ways we receive the gifts of the world, as we deliver *to* the world the gifts we bring from beyond it.

Think what a different self-perception that is than the ego's derogatory estimation of who you are. To the fear-based ego mind, you're a clump of clay that has to compete in whatever way you can for the material resources by which to survive. To the loving heart, however, you're a nonmaterial wave of energy, on earth with a spiritual mission. This mission acts like a magnet, making the forces of the world arrange themselves in a way that supports its achievement. No matter what you do, your abundance lies in dedicating your work to the purpose of healing the world. This is our common spiritual function, and it's only in performing our function that we can be happy.

We're not depressed because the economy is depressed; the economy is depressed because *we're* depressed. And we're depressed because we've lost conscious contact with the realization of why we're here. We feel it would be arrogant to think of ourselves as "God's gift to the world," yet in fact that's exactly who each of us is. It's humble, not arrogant, to realize this truth; we're not taking personal credit for the divine power that lies within us. Remembering that that divine power is there—in us, but not of us—is essential to the proper functioning of our mind and heart. Any thought or action that separates us from love separates us from our sense of meaning, our creativity and our joy.

You were created to live a life of abundance, with the support of the universe in carrying out your material endeavors. Nature itself displays economy, but not austerity. Yet many of us were taught—and by certain religions, no less!—to distrust abundance, leading us to subconsciously avoid or, at the very least, fail to develop the mental and emotional *habits* of an abundant life.

We need to do more than eradicate our thoughts of poverty; we need to allow ourselves to proactively embrace, to the point of embodying, the energies of abundance. To the universe, it's as easy to manifest six zeroes as it is to manifest two. As a child of God, all the abundance of the universe belongs to you, because it *is* you.

The idea that you must struggle in order to experience abundance—whether in the form of love relationships, money, or anything else—interferes with the natural magnetism that otherwise brings abundance forth. There is a difference between having to *work* and having to *struggle*. Work is creative effort, a righteous extension of positive energy that attracts abundance; struggle is a perversion of creative energy based on a misunderstanding of one's basic relationship to the universe. Anxiety and struggle do not attract your good.

If you think you have to struggle, you're forgetting your relationship to the universe; and the universe will then seem to forget its relationship to you! Your job is simply *to be,* joyfully expressing your own inner worth—and the universe will find a way to take care of you. But if you think, "I have to struggle, because otherwise I'm not taken care of," then your core belief is that you won't be taken care of—and you won't be!

The universe is programmed to support your happiness, and one of the ways it does this is by arranging events so that you won't have to worry about money. Why? Because you have more important things to do! That is the correct motivation for making money: so you simply don't have to think about it except as a tool for the betterment of all things.

It's difficult to open yourself to such thinking if you're not open to the idea of your own internal magnificence. Recognition of your internal magnificence is not ego; it's the acknowledgment of the spirit within you, which makes you no more or less valuable than anyone else. All of us are infinitely valuable to God.

Many of us were taught as children that we shouldn't express ourselves too much. We should pipe down in some way. Such children often become adults who are in the habit of cowering, as though we're afraid of taking up too much space. Our mind then comes into conflict with our soul's knowing. Because each of us is the center of the universe, we are here *to express ourselves,* and on some level we know this.

There is no need to feel you shouldn't take up too much room in a universe that is in fact all yours. You are here to fly at full wingspan, for the glory of the One who sent you. You give your greatest gifts when you are flying fully and freely. You're actually withholding from the universe when you don't.

If Mommy or Daddy or a teacher or a mate or anyone else you might have met along the way taught you for whatever reason that your job is to keep your head down, then bless them but know that they were misinformed. *A Course in Miracles* claims that those who have achieved the most in the world have achieved only a fraction of what each of us is capable of. And that means that you have as much achievement potential as any great artist, scientist, or anyone else who ever lived. Unlimited potential lies within you, just waiting to be activated by your own affirmative response to the idea.

Once you know this, you become a magnet for worldly success. You work from joy and the universe responds. You open your heart to love, and the way is made clear for you.

Love, in whatever form would serve us, is always coming toward us. Our job is not to go out and find it, but to allow it to find us. Money isn't just something we "go out and make"; it's also something we have to be able to "sit still and receive." The ego doesn't want you to believe this, but all you have to do is open your heart, and all the abundance you need will find its way to your door.

ONE MORNING, I was picked up by a car service for a drive to the airport. I asked the young man who was driving whether he was new to the company, as I hadn't seen him before.

"Yes," he said. "I just moved to Los Angeles from New York."

"Let me guess," I said, smiling. "Actor?"

"Well," he said. "Writer, painter—but I don't know. I do a lot of things."

I asked him what kind of painter he was and what kind of writer.

"I write dramas. But I don't know . . . I think I need to write something else in order to get something sold." He appeared to be struggling with his predicament.

"What does that mean?" I asked. "Like horror films or something?"

He nodded knowingly and rolled his eyes. I wondered how he was going to attract a sale by writing something he didn't even like to write.

"What I need to do is network," he told me. "I lived here before, and I knew a lot of people." He then rattled off some names of successful producers and directors, as though if only he had impressed them before, then he'd be living in Bel Air by now. "So I had the relationships, I just didn't know how to . . ." He moved his arms around as though to say he didn't know how to schmooze, to do the dance. He seemed to see this as the gist of his failure.

"But my real problem," he continued, "is that I don't know how to write a dramatic moment." How we'd gotten *there,* I wasn't sure. "I do have confidence in my craft, but I'm not confident in the art of it. I know how to write things technically, but I don't know how to write that big dramatic moment. I have to figure out how to do that."

"Well," I said, "I'm not sure you can 'figure out' how to write a big dramatic moment, because a big dramatic moment by definition doesn't come from the part of the mind that can figure things out. That's why it's called 'drama.' It has less to do with a rational formula and more to do with a spontaneous burst of emotional truth."

"Yeah," he said. "I guess . . ."

"So for that," I continued, "you'll need to learn to access your own authenticity and feeling. Otherwise, how can you convey it to others? I don't know how you can access your authenticity when you seem to think you should be someone other than who you are, wanting something other than what you really want, and doing something other than what you want to be doing."

"Yeah, you're right," he said, sighing. "I just gotta figure out how to do all that."

Oy. "Well, you're sort of doing it again. Maybe there's nothing to figure out here at all. Maybe there's just some insight you might want to let in. Your subconscious mind will do the rest. The subconscious is a better organizer than your conscious mind will ever be."

He is probably wondering, at this point, who the crazy lady in the backseat is. My cappuccino is kicking in now.

"The universe can organize itself. The embryo doesn't need to figure out how to become a baby. Buds don't have to figure out how to become blossoms. Nature has its plan figured out.

"Or you can look at it this way," I continued. Poor guy. I'm on a roll now.

"Think of a pile of iron shavings. Now, what's the best way to form the shavings into a pattern, using your fingers or introducing a magnet?

"Your internal self is like a magnet. Call it the Christ, or your Inner Light, or whatever; there's a spirit within you that naturally attracts all the patterns and details that would form your most beautiful life. Look what it arranged for you this morning!"

I laughed, as we pulled up to the Los Angeles airport and I searched the signs for Southwest Airlines.

"Yeah, I was thinking that . . . ," he said. "Now what did you say you do?"

"Oh, I just talk about this stuff a lot," I smiled, as I got out of the car.

The universe had indeed self-organized that

morning. The young man received information that might help him in his work if he was open to it; and I got a demonstration of how people hold themselves back by not remembering who they are, suggesting to me that I should include the issue in this book, thus adding to *my* work!

Yet neither of us would have been so served had we not been open-hearted and open-minded enough to engage in friendly dialogue with the person in front of us. He had introduced himself to me; I had asked him about himself. Those two things—seemingly meaningless moments of human connection—opened the door through which the universe could provide its gifts to both of us.

Neither one of us could get the gift, however, unless we made ourselves available to receive it. He could have been preoccupied and not at all interested in interacting with the client in the backseat, and I could have been preoccupied and not at all interested in interacting with him. These are the kinds of ways we turn down miracles all the time. We fail to realize that what we need is available to us at every moment. Most of the time, we block our reception of a miracle by believing it couldn't be that easy. But do flowers not grow easily? We think we know what we need, and what we need to do to make things happen. But do we, really? Just try strategizing a miracle.

People have no idea what they miss in life by discounting other people and the gifts they bring. In a universe where all is designed to provide us with perfect lessons in every moment, there are lessons awaiting us in the most unexpected places. Perhaps you've made the mistake of thinking someone "wasn't important," discounting that person in some way, only later to learn that he or she was exactly the person who might have helped you. Sometimes we're so consumed with "becoming successful" that we forget the importance of being successful human beings, of deeply listening to other people, of showing up spontaneously for whatever life has to offer. Those of us who have made that mistake have found that it wasn't ultimately good for business. My father used to say frequently, "Proud days soon pass."

There's no way to rationally formulate or predict where our next miracle will come from. In almost every moment, we're at the right place at the right time *if we step fully into the moment at hand.*

It's amazing how much our ego would separate work from love. We seem to think that success depends on what we do, but not necessarily on who we are. And nothing could be further from the truth. Anything that deters the flow of love deters the emergence of our success.

One common way that people deny the flow of miracles is by rejecting relationships on the basis that "I'm too busy with my career." There is no greater career than being a fully alive, fully present, and fully loving human being. Someone you're turning away from because the relationship will "take too much time" might be the one with whom you could have the experiences that pave the way to the very miracles you wish for. The universe doesn't categorize between "love" and "work," because in reality everything is love and everything is work!

Never think that turning away from love is a smart thing to do, or any sort of good career move. When you stop the flow of love pouring forth from your heart, you stop the flow of love pouring forth to your door. That applies as much to the flow of money as to the flow of anything else. Let it flow *from* you, and it will flow *to* you. Always.

CHAPTER 13

Meditation

Enlightenment begins as an abstract concept and then makes a journey without distance from the head to the heart. As most of us are aware, mere intellectual understanding is not of itself enough to change our lives.

Albert Einstein claimed that the problems of the world would not be solved at the same level of thinking we were at when we created them. The different level of thinking requires a different worldview, and different brain waves.

During our normal working consciousness, the human brain emits what are called beta waves. As we settle into meditation, the brain shifts and begins to emit alpha waves and sometimes even the deeper

delta waves. Delta waves help us access the uncon-
scious, reduce levels of a hormone called cortisol
(known to cause stress and aging), and produce a
restfulness akin to deep sleep.

**Just as we look to food to fuel
our physical selves, we should
look to meditation and prayer
to fuel our spiritual selves.**

True meditation practice is more than staring
into a candle and breathing deeply, sitting still,
slowing down our mind, and so forth. It is more
than deep relaxation. Deep relaxation is important,
but it is not meditation. All meditation is relaxation, but not all relaxation is meditation.

An actual meditation practice—such as going
through the Workbook of *A Course in Miracles* or
doing Transcendental Meditation, Buddhist meditation, or other spiritual, religious, or even secular

forms of meditation—includes a technique through which words or sounds instruct the mind to move into deeper regions. These regions hold the key not only to stress reduction but to much, much more. Greater insight, deeper understanding, expanded perspective, more whole-system knowing, and deeper peace, forgiveness, and love—all of these arise more easily from the meditative mind. The rational mind alone cannot cause these things to occur.

In order to not only conceptualize breakthroughs but to actually experience them, we need to embody the spiritual principles we embrace. We want not only our rational minds but also our spirits to be reignited. We want our psyches to be rewired. We want to experience miraculous shifts.

Such shifts are growth into our truer selves. Just as we look to food to fuel our physical selves, we should look to meditation and prayer to fuel our spiritual selves.

Meditation is like spiritual exercise, developing attitudinal muscles and making them strong. Consider it your daily workout. After a certain point in our lives, whether in relation to physical *or* attitudinal muscles, gravity pulls down what we don't work at keeping up! Flabby spiritual muscles are things like cynicism, negativity, victim consciousness, anger, judgmentalism, and fear. Just as we do well to exercise our bodies on a regular basis, we also do well to exercise our minds. As *A Course in Miracles* says, we are "much too tolerant of mind-wandering."

Meditation, again like physical exercise, isn't something we can afford to stop doing. We never get to look in the mirror and say, "I like my body now, so I can stop exercising." Neither can we say, "I feel at peace now, so I can stop meditating." Gravity, both physical and emotional, is at work every day. So should we be, in order to counter it.

Just as we wash to remove yesterday's dirt from our bodies, we meditate to remove yesterday's stress from our minds. A meditation practice is one of the most powerful boosts to our physical well-being, as well as to our mental and emotional health. It even helps us financially! According to an article published by the American Public Health Association, people who practice Transcendental Meditation spend 11 percent less annually on health care than does the general population.

Let's look more closely at how meditation affects our work and earning capacities. Today's work environment is routinely stressful. Between the twenty-four-hour blitz of often depressing world news and the economic anxiety rampant everywhere, many people feel like they're barely holding on. Dysfunctional responses such as overeating, drinking and drugging to excess, and self-medicating through recreational or pharmaceutical drug use have become common responses to stress.

Things are moving too quickly, and we simply weren't created for that. For millions of years our ancestors toiled with their bodies, worked the earth, and sat around campfires in the evening telling stories. They didn't fool around on the computer all day. Our challenge is to compensate for the wear and tear of modernity's assault on our nervous systems. With greater speed comes a greater chance that we'll make mistakes. We don't adequately think an issue through; we let fear rule a decision, digging ourselves an even deeper hole than the one we're already in; we fail to connect deeply with people and situations around us, leading to all manner of negative results.

But there is a revolution in consciousness among us, and meditation is at the forefront. More and more people are looking to nutrition, yoga, exercise, spirituality, and so forth to counter the dysfunction and stress of the times in which we live.

Years ago I had made a pot of chili. When I tasted it, it was too hot; clearly I had added too much cayenne pepper. When I called my mother and asked for help, she told me to put a raw potato in the chili in order to absorb the pepper. She was right: it worked! I never forgot that image, because it reminds me of how it feels when I meditate. Meditation absorbs my crazy thinking the way that raw potato absorbed the cayenne.

As a student of *A Course in Miracles,* I read one Workbook lesson every day—"I give my life to God to guide today," "Into His presence would I enter now," "I am at home. Fear is the stranger here," or whatever it might be—and while I can't say that the practice guarantees I'll be the best version of myself all day, it absolutely keeps me from being the *worst* version of myself. I might *have* negative thoughts or feelings, but the chances of my acting on them are drastically reduced. And all of us, if we're honest with ourselves, know how important that distinction can be.

It can take just one instant for a lack of impulse control to overwhelm our better knowing. We say something we later wish we hadn't said; we write an e-mail we later wish we hadn't sent; we respond to a text message we later wish we'd simply ignored. Or we simply weren't our best selves, diminishing the trust that others have in us. Those are the moments, not just in our personal relationships but in our professional ones as well, that can mess up even the greatest business plans and avenues to success.

The benefits of meditation go beyond destressing the mind; meditation actually *expands* the mind. It gives us insight and illumination. It builds wisdom and compassion. It goes a long way toward making us the people we wish to be.

Below is a prayer, followed by multiple statements that provide a meditative approach to money and career. Read each statement slowly, picturing the images it evokes, exploring the idea or scene, and inwardly asking for further illumination. You may make it through only one paragraph, which is fine. What matters is that we daily do whatever we can to realign our thoughts with the Mind of God.

Do the following meditation gently and without stress. Sit quietly in a comfortable position, close your eyes, and feel yourself in the presence of the holy. Open with a prayer, such as the following:

Dear God,
I give this time of quiet to You.
Please dissolve my thoughts of stress and fear
And deliver me to the inner place
Where all is peace and love.
Amen.

Then, keeping your eyes closed, allow your mind to gently switch gears. When you feel you're ready, look honestly over the landscape of your material life. With the power of your imagination, pour a holy light over everything you see. Ask to be shown all you need to see and know, and your spirit will guide you.

When looking at the subject of your work and finances, view them from the perspective of your spirit. Recognize your work as your ministry, and see ways that you could make it more so.

See what or whom you've allowed to go unnoticed, untended to, unappreciated, or undervalued.

Salute spiritually those you work with now, have worked with before, or might work with in the future.

Dedicate your work to holy purposes. See how the images change when you do.

Humbly confess and atone for any errors or financial irresponsibilities in your past. Ask forgiveness for any wrong-minded thinking, and pray for a miracle.

Notice any places where you are defended against wealth—where you feel it wrong or judge those who have it—and allow this wall of mistaken thought to crumble.

Now envision yourself as a person of wealth, expanding into the energy of abundance. See yourself gladly assuming the responsibilities that come with it. Commit within your heart that you will use whatever wealth comes into your life as spirit directs, as a means of blessing and never of harm.

See yourself in control of vast amounts of money, if vast amounts of money are what you truly desire.

See this money as an exchange of energy through which you bless the world.

For being, and having, are ultimately the same thing. *Know that whatever you can be, you can have.*

See yourself transforming into someone whose internal abundance aligns with a magnificent external abundance. Allow yourself to inhabit this space energetically, and hold the vision for a minimum of five minutes a day. Allow yourself to feel the subtle changes in thought, energy, feeling, behavior, and desire that naturally result from this.

Give thanks and praise God.

Amen.

CHAPTER 14

Prayer

In the words of *A Course in Miracles,* "Prayer is the medium of miracles. It is a means of communication of the created with the Creator."

Prayer is a conscious request that our thoughts be shifted by a power greater than our own. This shift from ego thinking to spirit thinking *is* the miracle.

A serious prayer life is a mental orientation—an attunement to God throughout the day. Prayer directs the mind to hear the voice for God over the voice of the ego, to notice the illumined thoughts and ideas that emerge naturally from the deeper regions of our consciousness.

With prayer, we're asking what we can learn, what insight God would have us receive, what wisdom He would place within us. The universe is like a house wired for electricity, but too often we're like unplugged lamps. Prayer is the way we plug in to the divine, aligning our thinking with the love that infuses all things.

The universe is like a house wired for electricity, but too often we're like unplugged lamps. Prayer is the way we plug in to the divine, aligning our thinking with the love that infuses all things.

Prayer expands our consciousness, thus expanding the set of possibilities that we experience. As we saw in an earlier chapter, when our attitude is negative, few opportunities arise. This is not because opportunities don't exist, but because our negative attitude and energy blind us to them. You might be sitting at lunch one day next to a woman who could provide you with a wonderful work opportunity, but because you're going on and on about how rough things are and how tough it's been for you, it doesn't occur to her to engage you in a conversation about professionally moving forward with her. For one thing, you've showed her how effective you are—or aren't—at handling problems in your life. Your energy deflected whatever miracle might have occurred.

If you had awakened that day affirming, "This is the day that the Lord has made"—a day of infinite possibilities because God is a God of infinite possibility, a day when the universe is reaching out its arms to provide you with every opportunity for joy—you would have been wired differently at lunch. That woman would have been blown away.

Your energy, your attitude, your positivity, your words, your ability to listen to others and truly dwell in the present—all those things make you a person others want to be with, want to work with, want to share ideas with. That energy is the spiritual basis of wealth creation.

I once knew an actress who was looking for work. She was constantly invited to parties, yet consistently turned down the invitations, saying, "You don't get work by going to parties." Boy, how wrong she was! You never know whom you're going to meet where, or what form an opportunity is going to take. The miracle-worker doesn't just show up for auditions; the miracle-worker shows up for *life*. And life reciprocates.

PRAYER RIGHTS THE universe around you because it rights your mind:

> *Dear God,*
>
> *I surrender to You my work and my desire for work.*
>
> *I surrender to You my fear, I surrender to You my money, and I surrender to You my debts.*
>
> *I surrender to You my sense of failure and I surrender to You my shame.*
>
> *I surrender to You my dreams and my visions and my hopes.*
>
> *Amen.*

That which we place in the hands of God is turned into right-minded thinking. The altar to God is within our mind, and that which is placed on the altar is then altered.

There is no magic formula for how to pray; no one is monitoring whether or not you "get it right." Simply pray from your heart, with sentiments such as "Dear God, lift all these things into Your hands." Asking that something be "lifted up to divine right order" means asking that it be lifted to the highest thought forms possible. A lower thought form is something like, "I'm a failure; I'm no good; I'll never succeed." A higher thought form is more like, "I'm a child of God. I know that I have made mistakes, but I atone for my errors. I'm willing in all ways to be the person God would have me be. I'm willing to be shown where I need to improve, and I know that God has a plan for me. I place myself in service to humanity, and I ask God to use me to help heal the world."

When we meditate and pray, we align our mind with God's power. Our nervous system takes on a mantle of peace; our anxious thoughts are replaced by peaceful ones. Our dull thinking becomes radiant and brilliant. And this corrective does not apply just to money or employment; it applies to everything.

Every single moment, every single holy instant, the universe is ready to begin again. The only time that God's time intersects with linear time is in the present moment; miracles happen not in the past or future, but *now*. Every single moment, God is pouring forth His love for you, with endless opportunities for renewal and rebirth. Every single moment, God is saying, "Here is the glory of the universe. Do you want it? Show up for it, because it's yours."

So we say unto all eternity, moment after moment after moment:

Our Father, Who art in heaven, hallowed be Thy name.

God, who dwells in the realm of Truth, may your Word be all-powerful in my mind.

Thy kingdom come, Thy will be done, on earth as it is in heaven.

May the world I live in here on earth reflect the reality of love. May I think Your thoughts, and make manifest Your thoughts.

Give us this day our daily bread; and forgive us our trespasses, as we forgive those who trespass against us.

Today, may I receive what I need. May my way be unblocked, as I unblock my heart to others.

And leave us not in temptation, but deliver us from evil; for Thine is the kingdom, and the power, and the glory, forever and ever. Amen.

And when I'm tempted into fear, may I be guided back to loving thought: that love might be my experience, and love might be my power, and love might be my happiness and peace, in every single moment of my day.

Amen.

And so it is.

CHAPTER 15

*Creating Wealth Through
Purity of Heart*

I once heard a story about an Indian spiritual teacher who told his disciples that their ashram needed a certain amount of money. When the disciples asked where the money would come from, he responded, "From wherever it is now!"

Wealth does not come from "somewhere else." It doesn't come from outside us, but rather manifests according to our thoughts. Money created righteously doesn't come *from* other people; it comes *through* them.

Looking to other people as the source of our money is an idolatrous notion, because it sees those people as the source of our good. It can also lead us to exploitative or manipulative thoughts or behavior. When we realize that the universe itself is the source of our good, we simply allow it to fill our needs in whatever way it chooses. And the universe would never exploit anyone. We do whatever it is we feel we're supposed to do, and the universe pays us in whatever way it deems right.

Purity of heart, then, is the miracle-worker's greatest engine of wealth creation.

Some things we'll do for free, because that feels like the right thing to do. Some things we'll charge money for, because—in different circumstances— asking for a righteous exchange of money feels like the right thing to do. But money itself should not be the reason we do anything. The universe knows what we need and is inherently programmed to bring it forth. It knows how to transform anything at all into everything that's necessary.

While reading *Cinderella* to my daughter when she was growing up, I was always struck by the deep wisdom that's in the story. The Fairy Godmother didn't order a new dress out of a catalog; she transformed Cinderella's rags into a ball gown. The Fairy Godmother didn't order a limo; she turned a pumpkin into a coach and mice into horsemen. Whatever Cinderella needed, the universe took care of it. Cinderella's purity of heart called forth the Fairy Godmother—that is, the spirit within—and the Fairy Godmother called forth everything she needed.

The Fairy Godmother's wand? True, loving thought. The light her wand casts onto things? True understanding. The magic she works? The miracles that result.

The Fairy Godmother didn't have to order a dress or call out for a car because the universe miraculously transformed existing material. That's how the universe operates: whatever already is, is the platform for what could be. Cinderella, despite her circumstances as a servant, had the mind-set of the miraculous. And so miracles came to her.

In one video of the story, Cinderella becomes upset after her stepmother and stepsisters have gone to the ball. She's on the driveway crying, when the Fairy Godmother finally appears. Cinderella exclaims, "Oh, Fairy Godmother, I thought you'd never get here!" to which the Fairy Godmother responds, "Oh, that's not true, or I couldn't have come." How metaphysical is *that*!

Our souls are Cinderella, the ego is the wicked stepmother, and the Holy Spirit is our Fairy Godmother. Each of us has a "wicked stepmother," i.e., ego mind, seeking to obstruct our good. And each of us has a "Fairy Godmother," i.e., Holy Spirit, working miracles to fulfill out heart's desire whenever our attitudes are pure.

According to *A Course in Miracles*, "Miracles are everyone's right, but purification is necessary first." There is only one category of impurity that keeps miracles at bay, and that is lovelessness. The Fairy Godmother didn't appear to the stepmother or the ugly stepsisters, because their thoughts were mean. They had plenty of material resources, but they did not have love in their hearts. Thus all their plans came to naught.

• • •

PURITY OF HEART, then, is the miracle-worker's greatest engine of wealth creation. There are three spiritual steps involved in the metaphysical transformation of lack into abundance: (1) be grateful for what you already have, (2) clean up whatever you need to clean up, and (3) allow yourself to want what you want.

The three together are a powerful brew.

1. Be grateful for what you already have.

It might be a platitude to say, "Be grateful for what you have," but it's wisdom nonetheless. It's one of those sayings we give credence to, but only casually. Most of us are grateful for many things, but in a shallow way. And shallow thoughts have only shallow power.

Given that one billion people on this planet live on less than $1.25 a day, most of us live a fabulously abundant life in comparison. Yet when was the last time we stopped to give thanks for the fact that we have a home at all? When was the last time we focused on something in our lives and really, truly gave thanks for it? When was the last time we made a mental list of our blessings rather than our grievances?

Giving thanks is not just a "nice thing to do": it's a metaphysical power, or "magic wand." By throwing the light of gratitude on what you have now, you literally increase its value in your mind. The universe then reflects that, turning your rags into a gown and taking you to the ball.

If your thought is, "All I have is junk," then you will feel that way. If you're grateful for what you have, thinking, "I have so much," then you will feel the plenty that surrounds you. And those around you will respond accordingly.

Lack attracts lack and abundance attracts abundance. If your core belief is, "I don't have enough," then you will never seem to. If your core belief is, "I have so much," then more will be given.

Could it be so simple? Yes. For such is the power of every thought we think.

2. Clean up whatever you need to clean up.

Most of us have had at least one unpleasant or even painful experience tied up with money. Someone may have stolen from you, or exploited you financially. Perhaps you blew a financial opportunity that came your way in the past. You may have bills you can't pay. You may not have a job, perhaps not even a prospect of one.

So what have we learned so far? We've learned that money doesn't come from the material world; it's a material thing with a nonmaterial source. When we have a money problem, therefore, it's a material problem with a nonmaterial solution, and the nonmaterial solution is in the mind.

I suggest that you make a list of all places where money is a problem for you. Write the problem(s) on the left side of the page, leaving several lines blank beneath each one.

Now do some serious introspection. For each money problem you recorded, write an honest appraisal of the situation in the space you left blank. Approach this task with an attitude of brutal honesty and commitment to truth. Taking responsibility for our own part in our disasters is critical to transforming them.

What was my part in creating the problem?

Whom do I need to forgive?

What remains to be cleaned up?

I've found this process revealing in my own life. While others have wronged me in the area of money over the years, a deeper look at the situations made me aware of how easy I made it for them to do so. Yes, they were perpetrators, but I wasn't a victim so much as a subconscious participant in some ugly dramas.

An agent stole my royalties; but, on the other hand, I hadn't read my own royalty statements for eight years. A lawyer failed to protect me; but, on the other hand, I didn't listen to my own gut, take responsibility for my own business, and speak my own truth. I learned how my own irresponsibility and unconsciousness helped create my financial disasters.

All of it was a lesson in becoming a mature and responsible adult, and I came to realize this. *A Course in Miracles* says that we pay a high price for not taking 100 percent responsibility for our experience: the price is thinking that we can't change it. Yet it was difficult to forgive those who transgressed against me without being willing to forgive myself.

To help with the process of taking responsibility and forgiving yourself, consider writing a letter to God about each of the problems you wrote down. Come clean about where you yourself made a mistake, didn't act in integrity, called forth fear-based responses by your own fear-based actions, and so forth. Allow your hand to keep writing, as He responds.

Be willing to hear Him, and make things right according to your internal guidance wherever you can. If you owe a bill, get on a payment plan. Even if each monthly installment is only five dollars, remember that the universe responds fully to that old-fashioned concept called "doing the right thing."

Once you recognize the Law of Cause and Effect as the basic building block of the universe, you begin to act righteously for your own sake. You realize that integrity is in your own self-interest. You seek to live a more impeccable life not just because you feel you *should,* but because you *want* to. You realize that the darkness in your life was called forth by fear, and you wish to be rid of your fear. The moment you enter the light of your spiritual reality, you rise above your ego and the darkness disappears.

3. Allow yourself to want what you want.

Many people have a hard time allowing themselves to really want what they want. They think, at least subconsciously, that asking for total happiness is asking for too much. They don't bother, therefore, to truly listen to their heart's desire.

But when your mind is attuned through prayer, meditation, and forgiveness; when your body is attuned through healthy nutrition and exercise; and when your behavior is attuned through a sincere effort at healthy living, then you've earned the right to trust yourself. For when you're aligned with truth, your desires are trustworthy. When you're praying and meditating, you don't *want* to judge and attack; when you're eating well and exercising, you don't *want* to sit in front of the TV and eat hot-fudge sundaes every night; and when you're seeking to live a life of integrity, you don't *want* to make money at the expense of others.

Desire is righteous when it flows through a righteous vessel. The righteous manifestation of money means manifestation brought forth by the right use of the mind. Righteously earned money is a reflection of the abundance you bring forth through the giving of your gifts to the universe. It is not in any way a bleeding of the resources of the world, or of anyone else's pockets. It is an expression of the Infinite introduced into the finite world.

In looking at nature, we clearly see its abundance. From the extraordinary design of a flower to the amazing colors on the feathers of a bird, from the magnificence of a mountain range to the sparkling light of stars at night, the universe keeps it simple in function, but not in presentation. That is how we should live our lives: keeping the function simple—serving the purposes of love—but expressing ourselves with whatever aesthetic or artistic sensibility gives us joy. The idea that only simple sackcloth expresses holiness doesn't jive with the natural expressions of a living, loving universe. Our outer circumstances do not determine the holiness of our thoughts.

Many people equate the love of money with greed, but no socioeconomic group has a monopoly on love. The love of money isn't of itself greedy, any more than love of anything else is greedy. Greed is when you have a desire that blinds you to the needs or wants of others. My love of art doesn't make me greedy; it doesn't make me plot ways to steal art from the walls of someone else's house. My love of literature doesn't make me greedy; if I read a book by Thomas Hardy, there isn't any less Thomas Hardy for you. Similarly, my love of money doesn't make me greedy, unless I'm thinking of my money as something I'm taking from you, rather than creating with you.

If I equate a love of money with greed, I'm subconsciously limiting my ability to attract it. For if I do attract it, I must be greedy; therefore I'm bad; therefore I must feel guilty; therefore I must keep money at bay in order to avoid feeling guilty.

And then we wonder why we have no money!

Now let's imagine another scenario altogether.

You generate righteous effort and receive financial reward in exchange. Remembering that all abundance comes from God, you realize that you are only the steward of your money. You realize that there is more than enough prosperity where that came from, because God is a realm of infinite abundance. You receive whatever is meant to come to you with gracious receptivity and gratitude, as well as a sober sense of responsibility to manage and use your money well.

Like everything else, money is a reflection of love. It is to be used as God directs, as a way to care for all living things. We are meant to use the money that comes our way to take care of ourselves and those close to us, as well as for charity and for nonprofit and righteous profit-making ventures. All those things, when done with love, further God's work in the world.

Money is meant to give increase, not only to yourself but also to others. You invest in a way that does good; you work in a way that creates good; you live in a way that feels good. And because of that, people whom you do not even know will experience increase in *their* lives that they would not have otherwise experienced. Someone's store is more likely to thrive because you shop there; someone's restaurant is more likely to expand because you and your friends eat there; someone's valid request for financial assistance is more likely to be met because you have money to be generous with.

You are empowered not because you have money, but because *with* that money you can help empower others. You're not coming from a "get" mentality; you're simply allowing the flow of universal energy to move through you and use you in a way that serves a greater good. Bless every dollar, and every dollar will then bless you.

CHAPTER 16

Working Miracles

One of my favorite examples of the Law of Divine Compensation is the life of the twentieth-century artist Henri Matisse. As an old man he had arthritis so severe that he could no longer hold a paintbrush. What a tragedy this could have been for one of the greatest painters who ever lived. He found, however, that he could hold a child's pair of scissors and use it to cut the construction paper that his grandchildren played with. This led to what art historians consider one of the greatest phases of his work: the Matisse paper cutouts.

Once again we see the difference between form and content. The fact that on the material plane—the realm of form—Matisse's hands could no longer work as well as they had did not mean that he had any less talent. In the realm of content, nothing had been diminished. Spirit created a way within the realm of form to compensate for diminishment and lack.

God will do His part
when we do ours.

So when we look at life from a spiritual perspective, we realize that the loss of our job is not the loss of our calling, and the loss of money is not the loss of our wealth. Our calling and our wealth, at the deepest level, are not of the material plane and therefore cannot be taken away. Do not let the appearance of loss deter you from the realization that what is given of God is given forever.

God has given you your identity, and that cannot be taken away.

God has imbued you with infinite potential, and that cannot be taken away.

God has provided you with the opportunity to change your thinking in any instant, and that cannot be taken away.

God has given you the capacity to love, and that cannot be taken away.

God has entrusted you with the power to live in the light of His abundance in any moment, and that cannot be taken away.

Even if we have only fifty cents, we can praise God and be blessed by that fifty cents. Even when we have a stack of credit card bills and accumulated debt staring us in the face, we can remember that in God all things are possible and that there is no order of difficulty in miracles. We can do the brutally self-honest work of tracing our own part, if any, in making the situation what it is. And we can atone, thus invoking the power of the universe to correct it.

It's a strong person who refuses to whine, who gets up even when he doesn't feel like it, puts his best foot forward, and goes to yet another job interview when he's been rejected by the last five prospective employers. It takes a person of real grace not to blame a spouse, or give in to "I told you so," or sit around and only cast blame on others for difficult circumstances. And it takes a spiritual seeker to realize that whatever is happening now can be a platform for a miracle.

God will do His part when we do ours. Even if we have only a frayed hat, we can still put our hat on and show up for life. We can pray for a miracle and think miraculously. Abundance and prosperity will show up when we do.

Today's reality is simply a mirror of yesterday's thinking. Now, in this moment, standing in the field of miraculous possibility, you can disenthrall yourself from the limits of your past. Nothing binds you except your thoughts; nothing limits you except your fear; and nothing controls you except your beliefs. Think God, think Jesus, think Light, think Love, think whatever form of divinity calls to you. And all else will fall away.

ACKNOWLEDGMENTS

Published books are a collaborative process, in which the author is surrounded and supported by a team of literary midwives. There is no way to overestimate the role of this support team in bringing a book to life.

I thank Mickey Maudlin at HarperCollins for his positive response to the idea of Divine Compensation. His organizing the transcripts of my teleclass in order to lay a groundwork for the book was a gift without which I wouldn't have been able to write it. I hope our association will continue to be both productive and fun.

I thank Ellis Levine for his wise and excellent counsel. I'm very grateful to know that you have my back.

To the brilliant, adorable, young-but-mature-beyond-her-years Liana Gergely, who spent many hours editorially assisting my process as I wrote this book, I bow in deepest salute and gratitude. As a summer intern who simply appeared "from out of the blue," she turned out to be a miracle sent from "a thought system beyond our own." I've told her this many times, and I'm happy now to have a chance to tell the world. She is one of those young people who give you faith in what the future can be.

To all the team at HarperCollins: executive managing editor Terri Leonard, production editor Lisa Zuniga, copy editor Kathy Reigstad, Kathryn Renz, and anyone else who helped make the book into what is hopefully a gift to its reader, my deepest thanks. Also, to Emilia Monell for final help with the manuscript.

To my friends Richard Cooper, David Kessler, Frances Fisher, Roger Wolfson, and Victoria Pearman, my thanks for the emotional support that only true friends can give. And thanks to Jennifer Ritchkoff for your willingness to share your story.

To Tammy Vogsland, Wendy Zahler, Drea Dauer, and Jill Angelo, my thanks for assisting me in holding the earth together while my writer's head was in the clouds.

To my daughter, India, there are no words for the love and gratitude I feel for who you are and what you are to me. As I've said to you from the time you were a little girl, it is truly an honor to be your mom.

To my readers and audience, particularly those at my lectures in Los Angeles, I thank you for keeping me on my toes. The depth of your searching, and the kindness that you show to me, are the inspirations behind this book.

There are others who have brought great light to my life, and you know who you are.

My love and thanks to all . . .

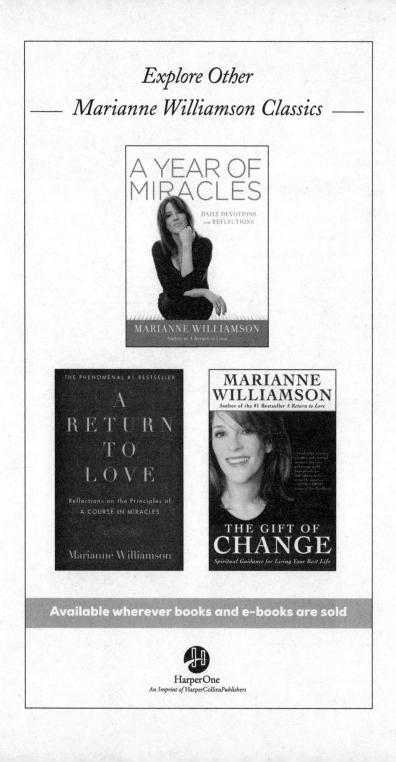